A Coaching Treasury
from the Basketball Clinic

Compiled by

The Editors of the Basketball Clinic

PARKER PUBLISHING COMPANY, INC.   West Nyack, N.Y.

Library of Congress Cataloging in Publication Data
Main entry under title:

A Coaching treasury from the Basketball clinic.

    1. Basketball coaching. I. Basketball clinic.
GV885.3.C62   796.32'3'077   74-7227
ISBN 0-13-139154-2

Introduction . . .

Here's a treasury of basketball know-how selected from over 400 articles that have appeared in our monthly publication, *The Basketball Clinic*.

Forty-five of basketball's top high school and college mentors combine to demonstrate (with over 300 illustrations) their ideas and techniques for winning basketball programs.

You'll find the best of offensive and defensive strategies, conditioning and drill programs that produce results, organizational tips that save you time and paper work, practice session ideas to keep everybody busy, and coaching philosophies that pinpoint the finer points of the game.

It's truly *A Coaching Treasury from The Basketball Clinic*, everything today's basketball coach needs to keep him on the winning side of the ledger.

Board of Editors

The Basketball Clinic

Contents

PART I OFFENSIVE PLAY (Continued)

PART II: DEFENSIVE PLAY

PART III: CONDITIONING AND DRILLS

PART IV: ORGANIZATION AND PRACTICE

PART IV ORGANIZATION AND PRACTICE (Continued)

PART V: PHILOSOPHY

Part I

Offensive Play

1

A Rotating Zone Offense for Junior High School

by Tommy Jones

Head Basketball Coach
Goodwyn Junior High School
Montgomery, Alabama

As head basketball coach at Goodwyn Junior High School (Montgomery, Alabama), Tommy Jones has a six-year record of 104 wins against 40 losses. This includes three city championships, one state championship, and two invitational tournament championships. His teams also placed second in the city twice and third in the state once. His record for the last three years is 56-18.

Our rotating zone offense is a simple pattern that constantly gives us shots of 15 feet or less—and is especially suited for junior high school play.

POSITIONS: We have a point man #1, two wing men #2 and #3, and two deep post men #4 and #5 as illustrated in Diagram 1.

The point man #1 lines up as close to the top of the circle as possible. He should be the play maker and the best defensive guard on the team.

NOTE: We prefer a right-handed boy at this position since a left-hander tends to pass to the left more than to the

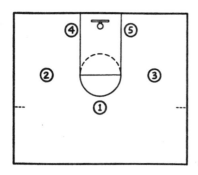
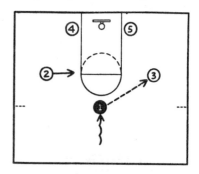

Diagram 1   **Diagram 2**

right—while a right-hander tends to be more ambidextrous.

Our wing men #2 and #3 line up even with the foul line halfway out to the sideline—although we might vary this against some zones. For example, against a 1-2-2, we might like them to line up deeper in order to split the gaps.

> **TIP: These two men should be the best outside shooters. We also want them to be able to handle themselves under the boards.**

If we have a good left-handed outside shooter we like to play him at the left wing #2 spot. Regardless, this boy must be able to use his left hand a good deal. We want a right-hander at the right wing #3 spot.

The two strongest rebounders are placed at the #4 and #5 positions. If we have a left-hander at one of these spots, we would rather have him at the #5 slot—as he would be turning into the lane to shoot and therefore, have better access to the backboard and also be closer to the basket when he shoots.

> **NOTE: As you can see, we don't have the conventional two guards, two forwards, and a center. Rather, we have really three guards and two centers.**

Basic pattern: Our basic pattern is illustrated in Diagram 2. If #1 is open, he shoots. Otherwise, he passes to either wing.

Here he hits #3, and #2 cheats in. #2 and #3 are responsible for deep rebounds on all shots.

Options: Any time #3 catches X-5 behind #5, it is an automatic pass to #5 for a turn around shot (Diagram 3). We insist that #5 square his shoulders with the backboard to shoot.

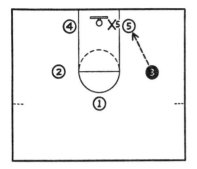

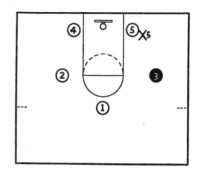

Diagram 3   **Diagram 4**

If #5 is covered, #3's second option is to shoot. As always, #4 and #5 are responsible for shallow rebounds and #2 and #3 follow for long rebounds (Diagram 4).

#3, being covered, whips ball back to #1 who shoots if open, or, if covered, passes to #2 or back to #3 (Diagram 5).

Rotation: We start our rotation as shown in Diagram 6. #3 dribbles to the baseline. #1 and #2 rotate. What happens next is determined by the defense.

NOTE: If neither X3 nor X5 covers #3, he shoots a jumper off his drive (Diagram 7).

If X5 starts out to cover #3, then #3 snaps ball to #5 before X4 can get proper defensive position. This is an especially effective option if #5 is taller than X4 (Diagram 8).

If X3 goes with #3, then #3 snaps the ball back to #1 who has rotated to the right wing spot (Diagram 9). #1 shoots if open or if not, relays the ball to #2 at the point for a shot.

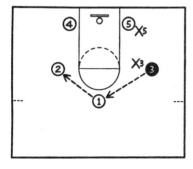

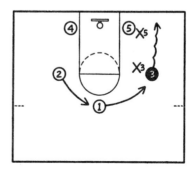

Diagram 5   **Diagram 6**

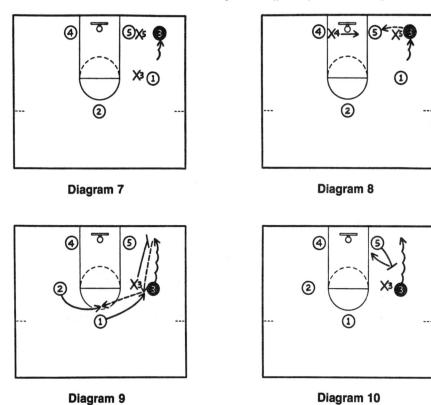

Diagram 7   **Diagram 8**

Diagram 9   **Diagram 10**

BEST OPTIONS: The shot by #2 here has been one of our best options as he is invariably open.

If #3 has an especially good jump shot and X3 goes with him, we like to send #5 out to set a pick-and-roll option on X3 when #3 is driving to the baseline (Diagram 10). Also #3 can drive toward the line, use a good head and shoulder fake and get his shot off over X3.

Any time #3 drives down and passes back to #1, #3 cuts to the opposite side of the court. If neither #1 nor #2 shoot, #2 takes one dribble to the left to create a good passing angle (Diagram 11) and hits #3 who shoots behind the screen of #4 on X4 attempting to come back.

NOTE: #3 can also hit #4 or throw back to #2 who has rotated and cut back to the opposite side to start the same options again (Diagram 12).

Comments: Of course, all these same options can be run to the left by #1 passing to #2 to start things. The pattern is simple, yet it constantly

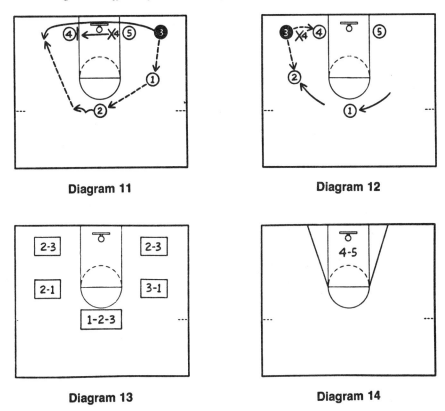

Diagram 11

Diagram 12

Diagram 13

Diagram 14

gives us shots of 15 feet or less and it is adapted to junior high school boys. We also run a few set plays that could have various keys. Sometimes, we will use a specific play to take advantage of an outstanding boy's talent.

> **NOTE: Sometimes, we hear of a team being right-handed, etc., but normally we get balanced shooting and scoring which keeps everyone happy. Over the last four years, we have had the following composite point averages from the five spots: #1 8.25; #2 12.25; #3 11.50; #4 10.25; #5 7.25.**

Balanced attack: It is easy to see what a balanced attack we present and when our substitutes' point averages are added, we get about 64 points a game. That we get good shots is evidenced by our team shooting average of 40 percent this past season, led by an outstanding 62 percent performance from our #5 man.

Of course, the offense can be adjusted to take advantage of an outstanding shooter by running the pattern more to his side. You can take advantage of an exceptional rebounder by running the offense to the opposite side to take advantage of his weakside rebounding—or you can run the offense to a particular side to take advantage of a rebounding mismatch setup.

Other advantages: This offense helps us in other ways also. Substitution is simplified. One reserve could play any of the three outside spots while another could play either of the two inside spots. One year we were fortunate to have a sixth man who could play any of the five positions.

> **NOTE: By having three guards, it helps us immeasurably against the press. Naturally, the extra quickness of three guards would also help us in employing the press ourselves.**

Practice shooting: The players practice only shots that they would expect to get in a game. Diagram 13 shows where each guard may expect to shoot. The areas of #4 and #5 as shown in Diagram 14 differ a little from the pattern we described in that they may change sides for strategic purposes. Also, before each game, one is designated to break into the lane if the zone opens up. The diagram shows where #4 and #5 do their shooting.

2

Massachusetts' Three-Forward Offense

by Jack Leaman

Head Basketball Coach
University of Massachusetts

*As head basketball coach at the University of Mas-
sachusetts, Jack Leaman has a seven-year record of 117 wins
and 62 losses for a .653 winning percentage–the most productive coaching audit in the school's history. During the last six
seasons, his teams have either finished first or been tied for the
top spot in the Yankee Conference five times. Coach Leaman
has received two Coach-of-the-Year awards, and has taken his
team to the National Invitational Tournament in three of the
last four years.*

We believe that any offense must be developed to fit the abilities of
personnel that will play in it. Any offense constructed without consideration given to the strengths and weaknesses of the players cannot be fully
effective.

**NOTE: We as coaches must make a critical evaluation of
the personnel on hand—and only then can we decide the
type of offense that will be most efficient for us.**

After a careful analysis of films and of statistical charts available we
made up our minds that:

1. We were strong at the forward positions with several boys between 6′ 3″ and 6′ 5″ returning with varsity experience.

2. We were without a proven offensive threat in the pivot position.

3. We had several guards who were strong in most phases of the game but were not high scorers.

THREE-FORWARD ATTACK: We decided that most of our point production would have to come from the front court—and since we have no pivot player, it was apparent that we would have to use a three-forward attack.

Research: After making this decision, we researched many of the fine articles and books written on offensive basketball (for example, material by Pete Newell of California and Ed Jucker of Cincinnati—both of whom had won national championships with offenses especially effective for front-court personnel). We incorporated many of their principles into the development of our three-forward attack.

NOTE: We're pleased with the opportunities this offense has given us. Although we have made some changes to fit new personnel, we are using basically the same offense we started with. In fact, we have now geared our high school contact program to interest players in our basketball program who would fit this type of offense.

Advantages: With this type of offense, we can be certain of good floor balance at all times. We can easily and quickly cover the offensive board and also allow for one and a half men to be back to provide defensive coverage to stop our opponent's fast break attack.

The three forwards are assigned to rebound position depending on their floor position and the position from where the shot was taken. The deep guard must cover the offensive free-throw line and the outside guard is the safety.

The offense can also control the tempo of a game. We can make certain we will get a high percentage shot while forcing opponents to play defense for a longer period of time—which we hope will have an adverse effect on their offensive performance.

NOTE: We can also force our opponents to defend in three different areas of the court. It is especially effective when we can force the opposing center, used to defend mainly in the pivot area, to come out and defend our smaller but quicker third forward on the periphery. This turns an apparent offensive weakness (no pivot player) into a defensive liability for our opponents.

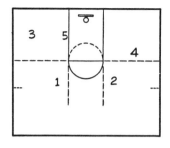

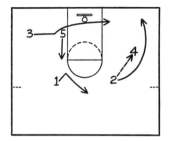

Diagram 1	Diagram 2

Basic positions: Diagram 1 shows the basic positions.

#1, post side guard, must obtain a position around the top of the key and about one step outside the foul lane extended. He must maintain a passing lane with the forward on his side of the floor and the other guard.

#2, entry side guard, must obtain the same position as the post side guard only on the entry side of the floor. It is important he keep open a lane to the entry forward.

#3, cutting forward, should line up on the same plane as the post to be in position to use this post to pick his defender.

#4, entry forward, probably should be your most agile forward. He must get a position about a step below the foul line extended and three or four steps from the sideline. This position is a must to open up the passing lanes to the cutters.

#5, center forward, probably should be the first forward down the floor. He takes up a position half way down the foul lane while facing in to the center of the floor. He spreads himself out to take up as much room as he can while setting a legal block.

Initial move: Diagram 2 shows the initial move.

#2 hits #4 and goes behind him to the corner position.

#4, after a fake to #2, takes a position and looks for the cutters (#3 off a screen by #5), (#5 stepping up to the foul line extended in the event of a defensiv switch).

#3 must set up his defensive man with fakes so he can be picked on the screen. He must time his cut so that he moves after the guard has gone past the entry forward. This timing is necessary so that the forward will be ready to pass the ball when the cutter breaks open. He can go over top or under the screen by #5 but must always end up in low post on opposite side.

#5, after setting his screen, steps up to the foul line extended and looks for cross-court pass.

#1 must time his moves to provide an outlet receiver at top of key area for #4 in case none of the options are open.

Continuity: (Diagram 3) If the ball is returned to #1 at the top of the key, #3 takes up screening position along lane; #4 drops down to set up his defensive man; #2 starts to recover to top of key; #1 makes the entry pass to #5—and we run the same thing from the other side of the floor.

> **NOTE: Notice the three forwards are now in different of-fensive positions causing their defenders to change their original defensive assignments. We can run this continuity offensive until the defense makes an error giving us a high percentage shot.**

Cross-court pass option: (Diagram 4) The cross-court pass to the screener stepping back to the foul line extended is the key for a change in the offensive pattern. This option is used to take advantage of a defensive player's trying to help his teammates stop the initial cut, or to set up a quick one-on-one situation.

Often we find this man open for a 15-foot jump shot. If the defender rushes up to recover, we have an unchallenged drive to the basket. I believe this option has been the most effective part of our offense. We can isolate any defender we wish and force him to play one-on-one defense.

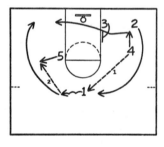

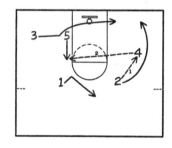

Diagram 3   **Diagram 4**

> **NOTE: With this offensive move, we feel confident that one cannot hide a weak defender against us. However, this option works even better against good defenders who are fighting hard to stop the initial move.**

Strong-side entry: (Diagram 5) We find that certain teams have practiced hard to keep our entry forward from receiving the ball in a favorable spot. We will then enter the ball on the post side of the floor and with one slight adjustment we can continue with our regular offense.

#1 enters the ball to #3 and goes behind.

#5 now reacts to this entry and moves across the lane to set a screen for #4. #4 cuts off #5 and we are back in our regular positions.

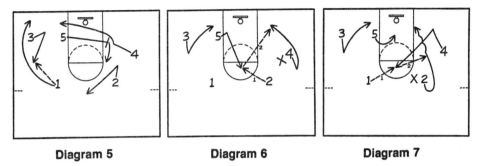

Diagram 5   **Diagram 6**   **Diagram 7**

Forward back-door trap: (Diagram 6) If the defense gives us undue pressure on the guard-to-forward entry pass, this automatically keys our backdoor trap for our entry forward.

#5 now breaks to the high post area to receive a pass from #2. #4 in the meantime is fighting his defender hard, taking him as high as he possibly can. As #2 passes to #5, #4 releases and cuts behind his defender to the basket. We hope to give him a little drop pass for an easy lay-in.

You don't have to run this option more than two or three times to relieve the pressure on the forward. A back-door cut will give the defender something to think about and very often will ease the pressure.

Guard back-door trap: (Diagram 7) Undue pressure on our guards at the ten-second line keys the back-door trap for guards. When the forward opposite the ball sees the pressure, he breaks to the high post area. As the guard passes the ball to the forward, the opposite guard makes a straight sprint behind the defender to the basket.

> **NOTE: We are looking again for a short bounce pass for an easy lay-in. Again, we don't have to run this more than a couple of times to ease the defensive pressure. No defender likes to be beaten for an easy lay-in; hence, he will ease the pressure out front to be sure we don't get behind him.**

Disadvantages: We don't believe that this offense is a panacea. It is not an explosive-type offense—and we don't get a lot of points in a hurry. Because of this, we often have to abandon it if we are behind late in the game. Also, we often keep weaker teams in the game for a longer period of time. This can on some occasions be very troublesome.

> **NOTE: To compensate for this lack of explosiveness, we have incorporated into our system a controlled fast break and a pressing-type defense. We use these two phases of the game for explosiveness, but basically we are satisfied to run our regular set attack with few mistakes and high percentage shots.**

3

A Simple but Effective Zone Defense

by Carroll L. Williams

Basketball Coach, Campus School
Southeast Missouri State College
Cape Girardeau, Missouri

For ten years of coaching at the Laboratory School of State University (with a small enrollment of less than 60 boys) Coach Williams has compiled a record of 135-101. Coach Williams is the author of "Coaches Guide to Basketball's Simplified Shuffle" published by Parker Publishing Company, West Nyack, New York.

One of the most popular zone defenses in our area is the 2-1-2. This affords good coverage both on the outside and in the center of the zone. It also makes the task of the offense much tougher than before, when the middle could be opened.

To meet the challenge of this defense, we found an offense that would be used any time we needed it with little or no preparation, other than the basic tenets of zone offense: good ball movement, player movement, short quick passes, and the percentage shot. Our basic setup is shown in Diagram 1.

PLAYER REQUIREMENTS: These are simple but must be met to achieve success with this offense.

Point Man: This man should be a sharp passer and a good shooter from around the free-throw line. He must be able to get the shot away quickly.

The point man must also be able to detect weaknesses in the zone and be able to attack them while on the floor, without waiting for instructions from the bench.

Wing Men: These men must be the better shooters on the club. If only one excellent shooter is available to you, place him on the right wing. These boys also will have to go to the boards when they are on the weakside wing, so they must be capable of rebounding. Their passing ability needs to be at least average.

Post Men: These two will have to be the rebounders and also good shooters from about five to twelve feet from the basket. They must be alert and quick. If there is a marked difference between the two, put the better one on the right side and allow him and the best shooter to work together on the strong side.

BASIC PLAN: This offense is predicted on moving the players and the ball into areas where the defense is not. We make moves along these lines and make the defense try to cover areas that they cannot get to as fast as we can with the ball. We stress the idea of floor balance and movement, and teach five basic moves to key the offense.

First Move

The first move that we make—and probably the simplest—is to pass to the right wing, our best shooter, and have him work for the shot on the slot or wing, while the low-post man on the strong side (X5) moves according to what his defensive man does (Diagram 2). If the defender goes out to cover the shooter, we dump-back a pass to X5 for the shot. If he stays in to cover X5, we hit from the wing. All this makes the defense concerned about the offensive power of the wing shooters.

Second Move

Once we have established the offensive effectiveness of this first move, we make a change: the weakside post man breaks into the middle (Diagram 3). Usually each team played will attack this offense differently, but most will send the top man on the side of the wing shooter to cover that man.

OPTIONS: As this happens, there develops a hole for the weakside post man to break into and have a good shot or a

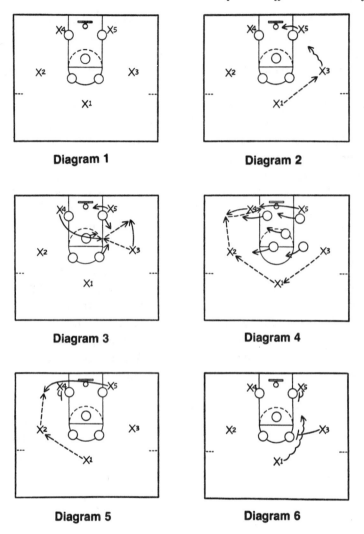

Diagram 1

Diagram 2

Diagram 3

Diagram 4

Diagram 5

Diagram 6

dump-back pass to X5 rolling behind the defensive man to the basket. At times you may have the defense collapse around the man with the ball, allowing a short pass to the wing man moving toward the basket for the shot.

Third Move

Another move is to have the ball reversed to the weak side (Diagram 4). The pass back to the point man is the key to a move that requires a little patience but is most effective. As we reverse the ball to the left, the defense, having seen what happens to the play on the other side, will usually jump out very aggressively to prevent the play from developing there as it did on the right. To meet this defensive move, we have the low-post man on the new strong side (X4) move out from the lane to a wide-post position and receive a pass from the wing man. He looks for the dump-back pass to X5 moving into the spot he just vacated. Usually X5 will get the ball close enough for a good shot and basket.

Fourth Move

When the defensive low-post man stays in tight to cover the offensive low-post man, another move results in a good percentage shot (Diagram 5). The low-post man on the strong side (X4) turns in and picks the defensive man, while the offensive man on the other side of the floor (X5) breaks along the baseline and sets up behind the screen for the shot.

ADDITIONAL MOVE: In order to get the point man a good shot, as we have for all of the other men, we have the wing man and the low-post man on one side of the floor (X3 and X5) simply pick in for him to drive for the shot off the picks (Diagram 6). This will usually work a couple of times during the game.

Against the 2-1-2 zone, this offense features ten points that make it an advantageous one for all levels of basketball:

1. *It is extremely simple for any level.*
2. *There is good floor balance.*
3. *There is player movement.*
4. *The offense works against a variety of defenses.*
5. *It can be taught very quickly.*
6. *Good percentage shots will result*
7. *Good inside and outside shooters can both be used to advantage.*
8. *There is good rebounding strength inside the offense.*
9. *This offense does not simply stand and shoot.*
10. *There is good use of the fundamental principles of basketball.*

This offense has produced results for us and will do the same for anyone using it in the prescribed manner. The term "unbeatable zone" may soon come to be the "unused zone."

4

Attacking Conventional Zones : ı

by Gene McBee

Head Basketball Coach
Columbia State Community College
Columbia, Tennessee

Gene McBee coached high school basketball for nine seasons in Georgia and compiled a 122-39 record. In three years at Columbia State Community College, Columbia, Tennessee, he has continued that winning pace. His first season resulted in a 27-3 record, a conference and a regional championship, and seventh place in the N.J.C.A.A. National Tournament at Hutchinson, Kansas. This was followed by 24-4 and 21-5 seasons with conference championships each year. His three season college record is 72 wins, 12 defeats.

In discussing conventional zone defenses we are talking about alignment of the defense into what is commonly called 2-1-2 and 2-3 zone defenses. We refer to these alignments as conventional because they are the ones most commonly used and have been in use longer than any others.

The normal 2-1-2 zone alignment is shown in Diagram 1.

The 2-1-2 conventional zone is designed to keep the ball away from the big pivot man, off the baseline, and generally in poor shooting position.

In placement of personnel, the two best little men are usually stationed out front in the number one and two spots. The idea is to be able to guard three or four offensive men with two defensive man, allowing the big defensive men to stay near the basket, stopping the drivers and being in better rebound position. The biggest and slowest defender usually will play the middle of the zone.

Diagrams 2 through 10 demonstrate the shifts of the 2-1-2 zone to the position of the ball.

Offensive Alignments Against the 2-1-2 Zone

There are any number of conventional zone offenses that have been used successfully in defeating the zone defense. Many coaches feel that the best way is to remain in their regular setup and force the defense to play them one-on-one.

This type of setup is shown in Diagram 11.
Some basic maneuvers from this setup are demonstrated in Diagrams 12, 13 and 14.

The idea is to spread the zone out as far as possible, setting up one-on-one situations inside. This is one of the most effective means of eliminating the two-on-one advantage that the zone is trying to set up. It will also enable the offense to exploit any individual defensive weakness that may exist on the opposing team, or take advantage of a strength the offense may have.

Forming Triangles Against the 2-1-2 Zone

One of the most effective ways of attacking the 2-1-2 zone is to form triangles that will give the offense a three-on-two or four-on-three advantage over the defense. This may be accomplished at any position on the floor, in order to exploit offensive strength or defensive weakness.

Diagram 15 depicts methods of placing offensive players to form triangles.

The triangle setup actually isolates two defensive men, X2 and X3, making their effectiveness in preventing passes or shots in the ball area nonexistent. In addition, any good ball-handling team should be able to get a good percentage shot from this setup. You may move your offensive alignment to different spots on the floor to form this overload triangle.

Diagram 16 shows how the triangle setup will give the offense a chance to work three-on-two or four-on-three.

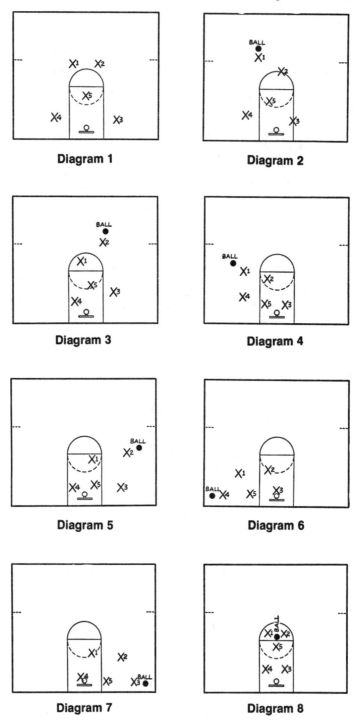

Diagram 1   Diagram 2

Diagram 3   Diagram 4

Diagram 5   Diagram 6

Diagram 7   Diagram 8

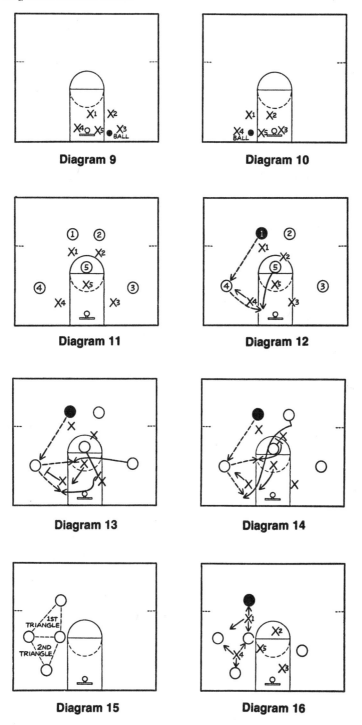

Diagram 9

Diagram 10

Diagram 11

Diagram 12

Diagram 13

Diagram 14

Diagram 15

Diagram 16

The 1-3-1 Triangle

The 1-3-1 zone offense triangle is one that has proven successful for many coaches. This setup enables the offense to hit cracks in the defensive armor and exploit the weaknesses of the conventional zones.

The regular setup of the 1-3-1 zone offense is shown in Diagram 17.

The offensive men are placed right on the perimeter of two defensive players' area of responsibility. This sometimes creates confusion for the defense, by making the defender responsible for the ball unsure whether he should go out or back to pick the man up or not. The alignment also creates passing lanes that are easy to utilize. It sets up four triangles of passing lanes that create a three-on-two offensive advantage.

Diagram 18 illustrates these passing lanes and triangles.

In Diagrams 19-22 you can see from where the good shot will come, depending on what the defense does.

In Diagram 19 wing man O3 should be able to get the shot before the front man can get back to cover him, if the baseline defensive man does not come out. If the baseline defender does come out, it frees O4 as shown in Diagram 20.

Diagrams 21 and 22 show where the open man would be if the defense made the two common adjustments to the baseline man.

The baseline man has gone out to stop the wing's shot, and the defensive pivot and the offside defensive baseline man have been forced to make one of two adjustments. These adjustments will leave one man open momentarily for the shot. These same options will occur when the ball is passed into any of the four triangles of the 1-3-1 zone offense.

Cutters and Screens Against Conventional Zones

Many teams use movement against the zones. One of the most effective moves is to cut a good-shooting guard through to a corner position.

This cut to the corner is illustrated in Diagram 23.
If this does not free the guard for a shot, the pivot man cuts to the basket as shown in Diagram 24.

If the pivot man's cut does not produce a shot, the pivot man clears out.

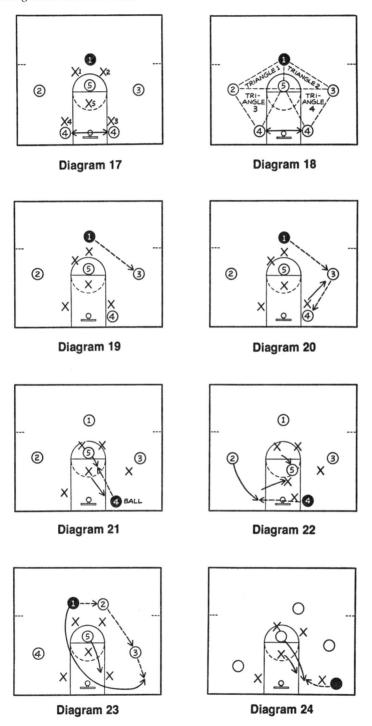

Diagram 17

Diagram 18

Diagram 19

Diagram 20

Diagram 21

Diagram 22

Diagram 23

Diagram 24

Diagram 25

Diagram 26

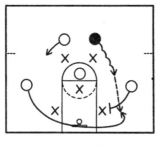

Diagram 27

The next move is a middle cut by the offside forward as shown in Diagram 25.

Naturally, this type of cut will be run from both sides of the floor.

One common screen-and-cut against conventional zones involves a screen-and-roll cut worked on the front-line defensive man and a brush-off on the pivot man.

These maneuvers are depicted in Diagram 26.

Another screening move is the cut by an offside forward and a screen by the nearside forward, as shown in Diagram 27.

These screens and cuts are designed to give good one-on-one offensive position rather than a completely wide-open shot. Not many fine defensive teams will give up the open shot, but it is relatively easy to set up your good offensive man or a one-on-one contest against the weakest defensive man.

Attacking Conventional Zones: II

by Gene McBEE

Head Basketball Coach
Columbia State Community College
Columbia, Tennessee

Probably the greatest single factor in defeating the zone defense is proper use of personnel. Time after time we will see good teams lose important games to underdogs because of improper alignment of offensive personnel. Sometimes you might have to switch starters or put different players into the game to get the most out of a zone attack.

> **NOTE: Many squads have a starting team against man-to-man defense and a completely different group to work against zones. Of course, it is much better if your five best men can be properly aligned so as to form the best zone offensive team also.**

Here are some tips in this respect.

Placement of Personnel

Normally you want to place your best ball-handling guard, who is not your best shooting guard, out front to direct the attack. This man should have the ability to see the entire floor to learn what is developing. He should be able to make quick, short passes, and above all have confidence in his ability to get the ball to the open man.

> **TIP: This confidence ought to be the most important qual-**

**ity necessary. A boy who has all the mechanical qualities
but loses confidence in his own ability will be a handicap.**

If this boy is tall he will have an advantage of being able to see over the
heads and hands of the front men—but size is not a necessary prerequi-
site. Ball handling, quickness, and confidence are most needed, for the
front man.

The wing men on the conventional zone offense sets should be the best
shooters. They are the men who will have to force the defense to come out
to stop their shot before the ball can penetrate the perimeter of the zone
again. A tall man has the advantage of being able to see over the zone, but
quickness in getting the shot off is most important. A boy who is set to
shoot before he gets the pass, and can release the shot quickly can beat the
zone before it has time to shift.

> **NOTE: This move not only gets a good shot, but it leaves
> the defense in the middle of a shift move and they will not
> be in good rebounding position. Left-handed shooters
> work better on the left against a conventional zone, and
> right handers are best on the right side.**

The best-scoring and strongest big man is more effective on the
baseline. Many coaches make the mistake of leaving the big man (6'6"
and up) in the middle of a zone where he can be double- and triple-
teamed. It is very difficult for a baseline man to be double-teamed. A
strong one-on-one offensive player who can muscle his way to the basket
is very effective in the baseline position against a zone.

The middle man in the zone offenses can be the weakest shooter or ball
handler on the team and still be effective. Of course, it is nice to have a
big scoring threat in the middle, but most teams are not blessed with five
great offensive players, so a coach must take advantage of what he has.
The tough rebounder is more effective in the middle because he is near the
basket where he can concentrate on the boards and also be a scoring threat
even if a poor shooter.

> **NOTE: The placement of personnel against a conventional
> 2-1-2 or 2-3 zone should put good ball handlers out front,
> the best shooter on the wing, the best scoring big man on
> the baseline, and the top rebounder and poorest shooter in
> the middle.**

Many teams will have overlapping abilities. The best rebounder might
also be the best shooter. For our teams, the baseline man has been the
most consistent scorer. He has gotten more good shots, more tip-ins, and
more follow-up shots. The wing men have been the next most effective

scorers, the front man has been fourth, and the middle man has been the least productive point-wise.

Passing Principles and Keys

The basic principle in passing the ball against a zone is that you should look directly at a specific defensive man and not at the offensive man. The offensive man is picked up by peripheral vision and a good passer can get the ball to him effectively without looking at him.

> **NOTE: This is one of the hardest things a coach has to do in getting his team to move the ball against a zone. The offensive man has a tendency to look at the other offensive man. When he does this he loses his overall prospective of where the zone is shifting to—and the result is either intercepted or deflected passes, or passes that are ineffective because the defense has the man covered.**

A passer who keeps his head up and looks at the defensive man will be able to take advantage of mistakes made by the defensive man and get the ball to scoring position more effectively.

Each offensive man has two or three specific passing keys to be aware of against conventional zones. Since we have determined that the passer looks at the defensive man we can now break down the shifts and see which defensive man the passer should look for. Diagrams 1, 2, 3, and 4 will show specific keys from each position on the 2-1-2 setup.

Diagram 1 shows offensive men 1 and 2 in a 2-1-2 offensive set keying the defensive man in a pass to the wing position.

Diagram 2 shows #1 and #2 offensive men passing to each other and keying the off-side front man of the zone.

Diagram 3 shows offensive wing man #3 returning a pass to #1 (front man) or #5 (pivot man) and the keys for each pass. These keys would be the same for the #4 offensive man with the keys becoming #2 and #4 defensive men.

Diagram 4 shows the keys for any pass from offensive pivot man #5. He must key the front man and baseline man on the side to which the pass is made.

> **NOTE: Diagrams 5, 6, 7, 8 and 9 show passing keys from a 1-3-1 setup against a conventional zone.**

Diagram 5 shows the point man (#1 offense) keying the front man and the baseline man on his pass to the wing on either side.

Diagram 6 shows offensive wing man #3 keying the defensive pivot on a pass to the baseline and the offside front man on a return pass to the point. The movement of the defensive pivot man will determine whether the offensive wing man makes a pass to the baseline or to the offensive pivot man.

Diagram 7 shows the wing man's keys on a pass to the pivot. These would be the same keys for the passes made to the pivot, point, or baseline by offensive wing man #2.

Diagram 8 shows the ball in the pivot. The offensive pivot man keys the defensive baseline man and front man in his pass to the offensive wing or offensive baseline. He keys both defensive front men in a return pass to the offensive point.

Diagram 9 shows the ball on the baseline and the pass back to the wing or pivot. The key for the offensive baseline man will be the onside front defensive man and the defensive pivot man.

NOTE: By following these simple passing keys and principles the offensive men should be able to eliminate most interceptions, deflections and wild passes. They should be able to move the ball quickly and take advantage of defensive mistakes because they are keeping their heads up and are able to see the open offensive man and the out-of-position defensive men.

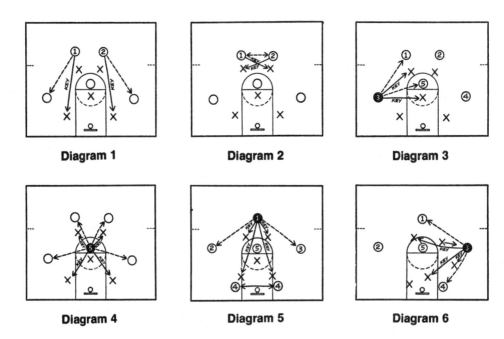

Diagram 1   Diagram 2   Diagram 3

Diagram 4   Diagram 5   Diagram 6

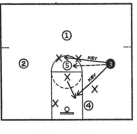

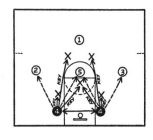

Diagram 7   **Diagram 8**   **Diagram 9**

Game Tempo Against Zones

The tempo of the game against a conventional zone will be determined by the nature of your team and their abilities—and the make-up of the offensive team. Many zone defensive teams are big and slow and stay in a zone where they are not easy victims of a good one-on-one or two-on-two offensive zone.

Other teams are small and quick and stay in a zone to be able to double-team big men near the basket and avoid losing the offensive advantage to the tall player. Still other teams play a zone built around a big pivot man to avoid fouls and to take advantage of his rebounding ability.

> **NOTE: Usually it is sound basketball to try to speed up the tempo of the game against bigger, slower teams. Obviously, if you can force the opponent to play a game at which it is not as adept as your team, then it is to your advantage.**

Many times you might have to employ a pressing defense, a fast break, and stress a minimum of passes before a shot, and driving to the basket, Not only do you want to force the big team to move quickly on defense—you also want them to shoot the ball quickly. This will many times leave them out of good rebounding position and will neutralize their advantage of height.

Against a smaller, quick team that wants to keep you from using your board strength and inside game, it is usually a good idea to slow down the tempo. You can slow it down best by playing a sagging and helping man-to-man defense or a zone to force the offense to take more time to get a shot.

> **NOTE: When you gain possession of the ball you will want to spread the defense as far out as possible and break**

cutters into the cracks and open places of the zone. Stress slow, exact passes plus patience in waiting for the shot. This patience usually pays off in forcing the defense to foul and to give up the easy shot underneath.

In the case of the team that is hiding a weak man or resting a good offensive scorer on defense, many coaches will try to get the ball in the area where he is playing—and draw the foul or at least wear him down by forcing him to play defense. Others try to work away from him and draw him into poor rebounding position. Both are effective ways of working on that type of defense.

NOTE: In closing, placement of personnel, passing principles and keys, and game tempo play a big part in attacking conventional zones successfully.

5

The Simple Way To a Winning Offense

by Edward J. Kuhnert

Head Basketball Coach
Freehold Regional High School
Freehold, New Jersey

In five years as coach of the Power Memorial Academy in New York, Edward J. Kuhnert compiled a record of 88-17, including four divisional championships, two runner-up spots in the Catholic School Championships, and a championship in the Johnstown (Pa.) Tournament. Coach Kuhnert's last season at Power was an undefeated 22-0 season, his squad winning the Catholic Championship and being considered by many the best high school team in the country. His overall mark is 105-33.

A coach is a teacher; his classroom is the practice floor. Success in basketball is based on a good knowledge of fundamentals, an unselfish attitude, and a desire to be the best. Like any academic subject, basketball must be taught from the ground up. Sometimes it's easier to teach a boy who is relatively raw than to reteach or unteach a boy who thinks he knows it all. The successful basketball program depends on how well a staff does its job.

Here is our breakdown:

FROSH	Fundamentals
	Man-man defense
	Basic offense (2-man, 3-man)
	Basic zone offense (stand-still type)
JUNIOR	
VARSITY	Fundamentals
	Zone defense
	Combination defense
	Basic offense (2-man, 3 man)
	Zone offense (moving)
VARSITY	Fundamentals
	Defenses
	Basic offense (2-man, 3-man)
	Special offenses

LEARNING WHILE WINNING: These are the basics for each level. The lower levels do add to them; for example, if our boys meet a pressing team, we want them to be ready for it, but we don't spend that much time on it. Our program is aimed at a winning varsity. We like ou younger teams to win—and they do—but we insist that they *learn*.

An integral part of our system, as noted, is the two- and three-man play. We use four basic plays and they are easily incorporated into almost any offense setup. Naturally, the type of offense used depends on the talent available. We attribute our success to consistency: with two starters over 6′6″ or with no starter over 6′3″, we have made use of these basic plays, though the offense would vary.

Give and Go (two men). This offense can be worked with any men on the floor, but usually we use it with two guards or a forward and a guard. It is probably the oldest offensive maneuver in basketball, but still is one of the best. A good chest pass starts the play. In Diagram 1, A passes to B and cuts away three or four steps. While A is cutting away, B moves away or fakes passing another way. A now stops sharply, pivots and goes hard for the basket. The idea is to get the defensive man on A to become lazy, cross his feet and lose a step. If set up properly, this play can produce many easy baskets.

EITHER HAND: Before using this play, a player must learn to shoot with either hand. In the diagram, A will be

handcuffed unless he can shoot with his left hand. In Diagram 2, we show the play with a forward and guard. Another important thing to remember is to teach the boys how to get open for a pass, how to receive it, and what to do with it when they get it.

Pass and Away (three men). Again a guard-forward offense. Essentially, the play runs this way: the middle man passes the ball in one direction and goes opposite the ball to set a pick for the third man. Good timing is essential; the third man must set his defensive man up by moving away from the ball and coming to it only after a block is set up. You will get many good jump shots from the foul line by having the man who sets the block pivot completely after the third man has gone through, and come to the ball. He often has an uncontested shot.

In Diagram 3, A passes to B, goes toward the basket and then cuts to C to set the block. He is facing the sideline—the broadest block possible. C takes his man away, then cuts off the block to the ball. The jump shot comes after C has gone through. In Diagram 4, after B fakes to C going through, A rolls back for the jump shot from the foul line. Diagram 5 shows the play with forward and guards.

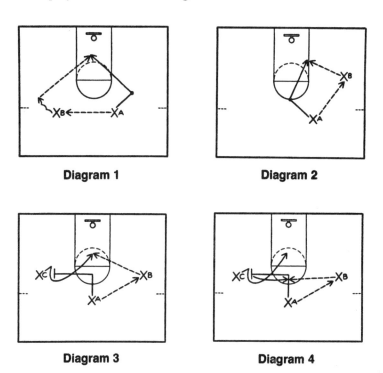

Diagram 1   Diagram 2

Diagram 3   Diagram 4

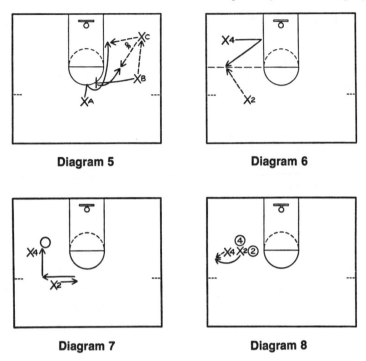

Diagram 5   **Diagram 6**

Diagram 7   **Diagram 8**

The Clear-Out (three or four men). This play was originally devised to free the pivot man for an easy shot around the basket. It may be used with a high or low post, or in a no-post offense. Essentially it is a blockaway from the ball for a big man coming to the ball. It starts with a guard hitting a forward who has come up from his corner spot to the foul line extended.

> **NOTE: The maneuvers involved in the exchanging of passes must be emphasized. In Diagram 6, X4, a forward, must move his defensive man in and out until he has him off balance. He then cuts diagonally toward the sideline. The guards exchange the ball until the right moment; they can cross and hand off, dribble or pass. We prefer to have our best all-around guard handle the ball, so we allow him to control it.**

When the forward has made his diagonal cut and has reached the correct spot on the floor, he faces the guard who throws him a chest pass. As soon as he receives the ball, the forward turns and faces the basket. X2, the guard, now starts his move; he fakes his man away from the ball, then cuts to it (Diagram 7) so as to end up eventually next to the forward. This can be dangerous if the defense decides to double up, but we have a remedy for that which will be discussed later.

In Diagram 8 we have the defensive men where we want them. Notice that O2, the man assigned to X2, is quite far from the ball. X2 now cuts back and around X4; they exchange the ball. Again proper execution is essential. A flip pass is used, with the forward pivoting and flipping the ball to the guard. If O2 is still blocked off, X2 can head to the basket along the baseline. We work with our guards on the sideline jumpshot, and this play has proved successful.

> **TIP: If O4 switches to X2 (Diagram 9), we send X4 to the basket to utilize the mismatch. Most often, when the switch occurs, O2 fronts X4. Rather than force the pass in, we are often content to let X2 shoot, with X4 having excellent rebounding position inside the small man, O2. If O2 doesn't front X4 we get the ball to X4. This is one option of the clear-out. If X2 doesn't go to the basket after the exchange with X4, then X4 does. He goes across the lane (Diagram 10) and establishes a block for the pivot man or corner man X3.**

X3, who has been moving his defensive man in and out, keeps moving until X4 has position, then runs the defensive man into the block. He may go inside or outside the block. If X3 is free as he comes over the block,

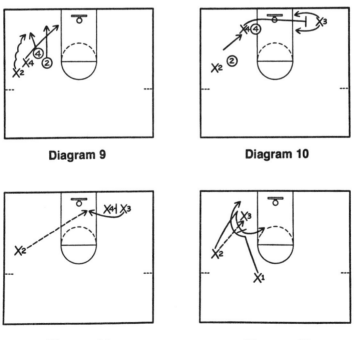

Diagram 9	Diagram 10
Diagram 11	Diagram 12

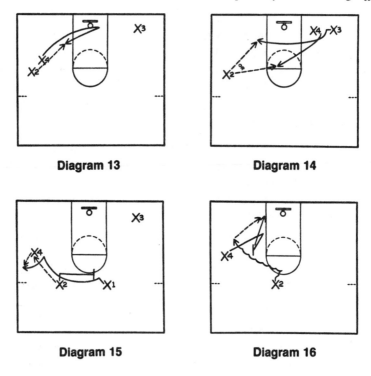

Diagram 13   Diagram 14

Diagram 15   Diagram 16

X2 throws an overhead pass high in to him. X3 should be able to catch the ball and spin either way for a hook shot or a lay-up (Diagram 11). If X3 can't shoot, he has the ball deep and the guards then split the post (Diagram 12). The timing here must be practiced. If the ball is thrown as X3 hits the middle of the lane, he will receive it on the ball side of the lane (probably too far away for a shot), and then we split him. The guard, of course, dictates the play by his timing of the pass.

> **COMBATTING THE SWITCH: Our pivot men and corner men are taught to shoot only if they receive the ball within the lane. Many defensive teams were able to prevent our big men from getting the ball by switching under the basket. We prevent the effectiveness of the switch by having X4 go half-way across the lane and, on hearing or seeing the switch, spin back to the ball—either getting the shot or establishing the low post (Diagram 13).**

Another way to prevent the switch is to have X4 set the block and X3 come across, but then have X4 break to the foul line. He often gets an uncontested jump shot (Diagram 14). We can also use this play as shown in Diagram 15. If our opponent likes to trap, this movement should make it a little tougher for him. Instead of X2 cutting to X4, he goes away from him, and X1 comes to receive a back pass from X4. This movement is a coupling of the pass-away with the clear-out. From these fundamentals, you will find many options of your own.

Up-Block (two men). In basic basketball language our up-block is the pick and roll. If it can work in the pros (as with the New York Knicks) it can work in high school. We have found this move most successful with a one-guard offense (Diagram 16). The forward breaks out to the foul line extended near the three-second lane. He faces the sideline to offer the broadest block. The guard moves his defensive man away from the block, then directly into it. He must force his man into the block, causing a momentary lapse in defense. The guard can then go all the way in for a lay-up or stop at the baseline for a jump shot.

If the defense switches, the guard tries to keep the defensive forward on him, allowing our forward to take advantage of a mismatch close to the basket. As seen in the last diagram (17), the block is set with the forward

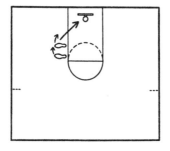

Diagram 17

facing away from the play. If a switch occurs, this allows him to go directly to the basket with only a half pivot. If run properly, this play can help win games.

> **PROPER EXECUTION can make even the simplest offense a winner. It is the result of endless hours of practice coupled with a thorough training in fundamentals. A coach who believes in his players and who has his players believe in him will be successful. Complete cooperation between player and coach is essential. This is where patience and pride become prime ingredients.**

Probably the greatest winners in sports history were the Boston Celtics. Their immense pride was one thing that put them above other teams. The Celtics had only a few basic plays (with options), but perfect execution enabled them to catch their opponents off guard constantly. High school basketball is a game, and the players should enjoy it. A few simple plays, with perfect execution, will allow a boy to keep his mind on the game, enjoy it and also *win*. If the coach has taught well, he'll produce a winner. Like a good teacher, a good coach knows how to get the best from his men. The coach must adapt to his personnel, know when to criticize, and most of all, when to praise.

6

Out-of-Bounds Plays: An Easy Two

by Gus Pappas

Retired Basketball Coach
Glendale High School
Glendale, Arizona

Gus Pappas coached high school basketball for over ten years in the states of Iowa and Arizona. His overall record is 138 wins against 34 losses, and includes an undefeated season and seven district championships. At present, he is retired from the coaching field, and teaching at Glendale.

Most basketball coaches have the philosophy that on an out-of-bounds play the objective is to get the ball in-bounds without having it intercepted by the opponents. This writer agrees with this theory—but to the greedy coach, the offensive team is in an advantageous position to score a quick basket by using an out-of-bounds play.

> **NOTE: Thus, retaining control is not the objective—to score is the goal. Because the defense is usually standing still, with little idea as to the offensive's next move, it is ideal to take advantage of the situation.**

Some Background

Out-of-bounds plays occur in about the same proportion as held balls.

In checking over past statistics, a coach would notice that usually between four and ten times per game his team was awarded the ball under their goal. Without a play a simple throw-in would be used to control the ball.

> **NOTE: Why not try to score an additional eight to twenty points per game? A quick score from an out-of-bounds play shakes the confidence of opponents and increases the scoring team's spirit and morale. Can't you remember a cluster game where you either won or lost because you did or didn't have an effective out-of-bounds play?**

In my coaching experience, many games were won due to the success of a score or several scores from well-executed out-of-bounds plays during the clutch game. This was sufficient reason for devoting eight minutes each day to practice this phase of the game.

Plays from Same Offensive Alignment

In order to obtain success with the out-of-bounds plays, it's necessary to have several under-the-basket plays from the same offensive alignment. The plays should be utilized throughout the season, with plays being changed at half-time and before the opponent reappears on your schedule.

> **NOTE: The ones we have used all provided a good shot and had movement in several directions with a safety man acting as a defensive safety.**

Personnel

The player who takes the ball out-of-bounds should be a good rebounder, cool headed and an accurate passer. It's best to use the same man each time the opportunity exists. This will cut down confusion in the players' minds and speed setting up for the play. The out-of-bounder is told to keep the ball moving, faking right and left and up and down—and avoiding telegraphing his initial pass.

> **SIGNAL: Some sort of a signal should be used to initiate the movement of the players and the pass of the ball in court. It was our desire to call the play number, and each player began to count when the referee handed the ball to the out-of-bounds player. When the count reached *three* the players initiated their movements.**

Some coaches prefer slapping the ball, raising the ball in the air, or giving a name or number to initiate movement. Whatever signal is used, timing becomes essential and this means practice is necessary to attain success.

NOTE: Basically all out-of-bounds plays work best against a man-for-man defense. But they are also effective against zones. Five out-of-bounds plays that have worked well for us are described and illustrated in the following paragraphs.

Basic Alignment

Diagram 1 illustrates the basic alignment. All plays may be run from either side of the basket, utilizing the same alignment.

The line formation shows the offensive players who are in-bounds, facing O5 who has the ball out-of-bounds. Each member stands close to another. It must be assumed that the defense is obliged to place one man, X2, on the side of the play to prevent O2, O3 or O4 from cutting to this spot for a pass in and a short jump shot (Diagram 2).

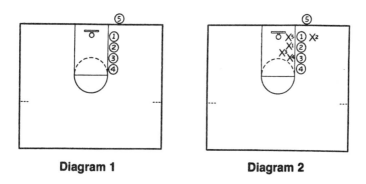

Diagram 1   Diagram 2

5 Basic Plays

1. Play number one illustrated in Diagram 3 shows players breaking according to their numbers to the indicated spots: O1 goes first; then O2, etc.

NOTE: O5 will step into rebound position after the pass to one of the breaking men. O5 will have four possibly open men to pass to for a good shot.

2. Diagram 4 shows O1 setting a pick on O2's man. O2 breaks off to

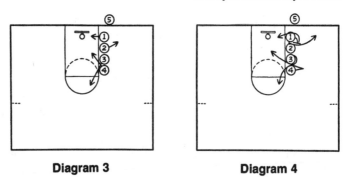

Diagram 3   **Diagram 4**

the right and if he is open receives the in-pass from O5. O1 rolls off his screen and may be open as he steps into a rebounding position.

> **NOTE: Oftentimes O2 finds O1 open and passes to him for the close-in shot. O3 pivots and breaks back as the safety man. On the pivot, O4 then faces right and cuts to the key area. O5 will make the pass and break to his rebounding position.**

Thus, several possible pass-ins occur as all four men break simultaneously.

3. Play three (Diagram 5) finds O2 faking right and sliding across the key. At the same time, O1 sets a pick on O3. O3 cuts off the pick and O1 rolls down after his pick. O5 may hit O2, O3 or O1 in that sequence. O4 again moves back as the safety man.

4. Diagram 6 illustrates the fourth play with O4 lining up on either side of the line. O4 is instructed to run his man into the screen formed by O3. Then O2 breaks to the side opposite the one to which O4 goes. O3 then becomes the defensive safety while O1 and O5 move into rebound positions.

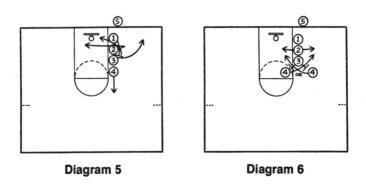

Diagram 5   **Diagram 6**

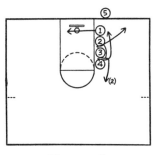

Diagram 7

5. The fifth play as shown in Diagram 7 finds O1 breaking left and going under and to the side of the basket. O3 breaks to the right toward the baseline. O2 times his move and sets a screen on O4. O4 comes off the screens and down the outside line, with O2 remaining back as the defensive safety.

> **NOTE: O2 can also roll after the screen. The player taking the ball out-of-bounds again has four options for his initial pass.**

Conclusion

The result of our success in scoring from our out-of-bounds plays has produced players who believe that we have an easy two points each time the ball is ours on the baseline under the basket. This type of confidence has been the difference between victory and defeat in many of our close games.

7

A Disciplined Offense with Freedom of Movement

by Leo Anthony

Head Basketball Coach
Princess Ann High School
Virginia Beach, Virginia

The basketball team at Princess Anne High School (Virginia Beach, Virginia), under head coach Leo Anthony, is rapidly gaining the reputation of being one of the best disciplined in high school circles. In his first year, 1968-69, his squad compiled a 13-5 record; in 1969-70, the Cavaliers were 16-4; in 1970-71, they were 18-4 and Eastern Regional runners-up; they started the 1971-72 season with 12 straight victories and ended up with a record of 15-3. Last season, they finished with a 16-4 record and the Christmas Classic championship.

My offensive philosophy is quite simple—we try to get the ball up the court as quickly as possible, attempting to score before the defense is set. If the defense is ready, we will then go into our set offense. We stress the following:

1. Don't dribble until you're ready to go someplace. Don't get into the habit of bouncing the ball as soon as you receive it.

2. Make your individual move or pass within three seconds.

3. When you don't have the basketball, work for position. Keep moving.

4. As soon as you get the ball, *turn and face the basket* to take advantage of any defensive lapse.

5. These three things have to be done in three seconds or less: pass to teammate who is open; take a shot or make an individual offensive move; dribble.

Free-Lance Play

We will run a certain amount of free-lance offense in every game. But we don't believe in a complete game being played in this manner. We believe in a disciplined offense with freedom of movement—and here's how we run such an offense.

Double-Post Offense

Diagram 1 shows our basic set-up. We have a point man, X1; two wingmen, X2 and X3; and two post men, X4 and X5.

NOTE: At times, we will have our wingmen line up behind the post and break to their positions (Diagram 2).

Circle Pattern

Our first play pattern is designed primarily to get the ball into our post men. I call it the "circle" pattern. It should be kept in mind that all my patterns can be run from either side.

EXECUTION: As shown in Diagram 3, X1 passes to X3 and interchanges with X2—and X4 clears to the other side. X3 or X4, depending on who has the ball, tries to get it into X5.

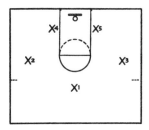 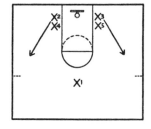 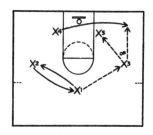

Diagram 1   **Diagram 2**   **Diagram 3**

This simple maneuver has been good to us. Actually, all we have done is to take away the defensive help on our pivot and force the defensive man to declare himself. If he plays in front or on the side, we can lob the ball to our center. If he plays behind, we can get the ball in close for a one-on-one situation.

Shuffle Option

If X3 passes the ball back to X2, we are in our shuffle option (Diagram 4). X5 moves up along the free-throw lane; X2 passes to X1; and X3 tries to rub his man off on X5. X2, after making his pass to X1, screens for X5; and X5 becomes the second option.

NOTE: If none of these options is open, we will free-lance until we get a chance to set up again.

Pick-and-Roll

Our second play pattern is designed to force a smaller defensive player to switch and guard one of our big post players. X5 comes up and sets a pick on X1's defensive man. X3 clears to the other side and comes around a double screen set by X2 and X4.

NOTE: X1 has his choice of executing a pick and roll (Diagram 5) with X5 or reverse dribble and pass to X3 for a shot behind the double screen (Diagram 6).

      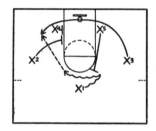

Diagram 4   Diagram 5   Diagram 6

Double Screen

Another play pattern that has given us good results has been the double screen for the center and its options. X1 passes to X2; X2 passes back to X1 and sets a pick for X1. X4 comes around the double screen set by X3 and X5. X1 can pass to X4 coming around the double screen (Diagram 7), or he can execute a roll-off maneuver with X2 (Diagram 8).

Blind-Cut Play Pattern

Our fourth play pattern was designed to take advantage of teams that are pressuring our wingmen. Whenever our center sees the defensive man playing our wing tight, he will break up to the high-post position, and this is the signal to run our blind-cut play pattern.

> **EXECUTION: X1 will pass to X5 breaking to the high-post position, and X3 will set his man up by taking a step toward X1. Then, suddenly, X3 will change direction and quickly break to the basket. X5 can hit him with a quick bounce pass, if he is open, or hand off to X1 for a jump shot or layup depending upon the reaction of the defense. X5 can wheel and go to the basket or take a jump shot any time he sees the opportunity (Diagram 9).**

Offensive Philosophy

Our first attempt, as stated in the beginning of this article, is to get the ball up the court as quickly as possible, attempting to score before the defense is set. We do this from our disciplined fast break.

> **NOTE: As you've already gathered, my entire coaching viewpoint is centered around the word *discipline*. I would attribute my whole success as a player and a coach to this philosophy.**

Disciplined Break

We go right into our offensive set if we do not get the break. See Diagram 10.

X1 = point man, *always* gets the ball around the key or maneuvers to get open in foul lane area.

X2 = always goes to left lane no matter where he is on floor.

X3 = always goes to right lane.

X4 = trailer on left side.

X5 = trailer on right side.

> **NOTE: Rebounder is always safety trailer.**

We have wrinkles we put in if they try to defense our original break.

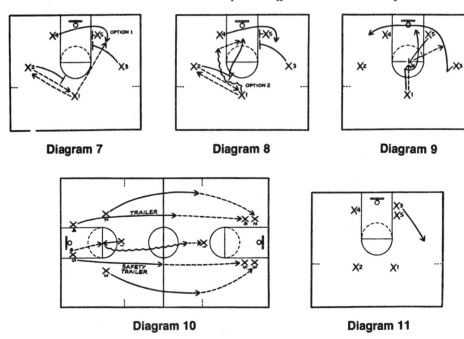

Diagram 7   **Diagram 8**   **Diagram 9**

Diagram 10   **Diagram 11**

Our men go right into our 4 or 3 stack set if we cannot get a good shot on the break.

Individual Offense

Our players must memorize and master these rules or they are not allowed to play or be a part of our disciplined team:

1. *Without the ball*
   a. rules
      1. move to be a good receiver—move toward the pass
      2. don't stand
      3. set up defensive man with a good fake before moving to be receiver
      4. head hunt when setting a screen; don't screen an area, screen a man
      5. when overplayed make a hard cut for the basket (backdoor)
      6. when clearing for dribbler always look for the ball
      7. when screening roll toward the basket and look for return pass
      8. post men lock defensive man with body position
      9. keep your defensive man busy, don't let him get set—entertain him
      10. If name is called, cut for basket

2. *With the ball*
   a. rules
      1. assume the triple threat position as soon as you receive the ball
      2. from the triple threat position, drive, shoot, or pass
      3. pass the ball and move, don't stand.
   b. moves
      1. jab or delay step and explode
      2. cross-over step
      3. wing drive
      4. cross over and shoot jump shot by planting inside foot
      5. rocker step
      6. step away from dribble
      7. reverse dribble
      8. dribble screen, head hunt defensive man, screen and roll toward the basket
      9. post moves—same basic moves
    10. drop weight prior to pivot move
    11. saddle move to basket
    12. snake move to basket
    13. drop-step move
    14. reverse
    15. behind-the-back dribble
    16. through-the-legs dribble (inside out)
    17. stagger dribble

Disciplined Offense (3 Stack)

We also use this disciplined offense from a 3 stack set (Diagram 11). We bring X2 out and play a 2-guard set. We flip-flop our offense to either side. We run the identical patterns that we use in our 4 stack.

Conclusion

Although our offense seems very disciplined, it allows freedom of offensive movement and allows a player with great offensive potential to take advantage of any given situation.

For example: In 1969-70, Rickey Michaelsen, our All-American forward, averaged 39.6 points per game—first in the state and third in the country. In 1970-71, Tommy Butts, a junior, led our team in scoring with a 23.6 average. He was third in the state and first in the Eastern Region. Tommy led us to Eastern Region runner-up with a 20-5 record.

8

Clear Outs Used with the Basic Shuffle

by Bob Wachs

Head Basketball Coach
Northern State College
Aberdeen, South Dakota

Bob Wachs has been coaching basketball at Northern State College for the past 18 years. His record is 311 wins against 158 losses.

Our basic working formation for our shuffle offense and our clear outs is shown in Diagram 1. We try to teach all of our men to run all spots in our shuffle offense except the post position.

NOTE: We enter our basic working formation in three different ways. These ways (or series) might vary from game to game, half to half; or in certain situations we might use only one series. Sometimes the defense might dictate that series is best or we might use one series more in one game because we want certain individuals in specific spots.

We start all of our series from the tandem formation. Diagram 2 shows the tandem right formation; we also start from tandem left.

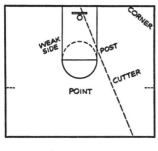

Diagram 1

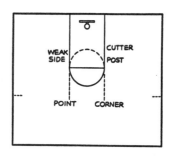

Diagram 2

10 Series

We use the 10 series more than any of the others. We call the man bringing the ball down the court our corner man. The corner man brings the ball up and moves it to the cutter breaking to his spot. The corner man then moves to the corner position and the point moves over.

NOTE: Diagram 3 shows the 10 series movement to the basic working formation.

20 Series

In the 20 series, the corner man dribbles over to the cutter's position; cutter breaks to the corner, and they now exchange names and positions. We are now in our basic working formation.

NOTE: Diagram 4 shows the 20 series movement to the basic working formation.

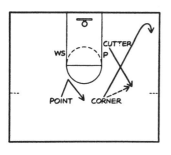

Diagram 3

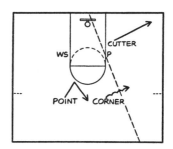

Diagram 4

30 Series

As the corner guard is bringing the ball up the court, the point guard goes to the corner as the ball is about to be entered into the cutter. Now the point and corner exchange positions. The basic working formation has now been established.

NOTE: Diagram 5 shows the 30 series movement to the basic working formation.

Basic Working Formation, Left Side

We also have our basic working formation on the left side. If for example the corner man is bringing the ball down the right side but is pressured and the defense forces us to enter on the weak side, the post just moves over and the weak side (ws) and cutter exchange positions and duties.

NOTE: Diagram 6 shows the 10 series movement on the weak side.

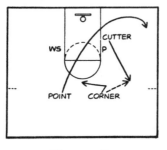
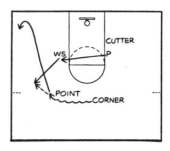

Diagram 5   Diagram 6

Now our basic working formation is the left side. The weak side is the cutter and the cutter becomes the weak side. Our point can very easily become the weak side by just moving and interchanging on the weak side. We do this because of pressure or just to exchange positions.

Shuffle Cut

Our shuffle cut is no different from that used by many other teams. We try to use the post as a second option for our weak side to hit. After the cutter moves the ball to the point, he walks his man into the post, and looks for the ball from the weak side who has received it from the point. Our post follows the cutter across for the rebound or a pass from the weak side.

NOTE: Diagram 7 shows the passing options of the weak side when he receives the ball. To get some movement, we now have the point and corner exchange positions.

Clear Out Situations

One of the clear out situations that has developed for us is when the weak side can't hit either option in Diagram 7. If the weak side doesn't hit either option as mentioned, the corner receives the ball as shown in Diagram 8.

NOTE: Diagram 8 also shows the position of all five men.

Now the point breaks straight out to receive the ball from the corner man. From this spot we try to do two basic things. First, the side has been cleared for the point to do what he desires—drive or shoot. At the same

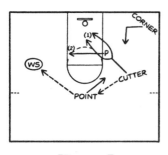

Diagram 7

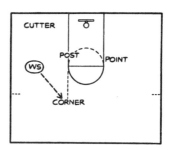

Diagram 8

time, we are trapping and trying to box in the cutter's defensive man. The weak side picks at him and the corner man goes straight down the lane to jam it up. If the clear out man doesn't drive or shoot he looks for the cutter.

NOTE: Diagram 9 shows movement of men when point receives the ball.

A second clear out situation we use is before the shuffle cut. This clear out has to be pre-planned such as on baskets made, out-of-bounds, free throws made or missed, etc.

TIP: Naturally, the situation can be taken off or put on at any time during a game.

Clear Out Techniques

The clear outs start and look just like the regular pattern. The point receives the ball in the middle of the court from the cutter; weak side breaks out for the pass; point fakes pass to him—meanwhile the cutter is walking his man into the post and the corner is clear out.

NOTE: Diagram 10 shows movement as point receives the ball and gets ready to drive.

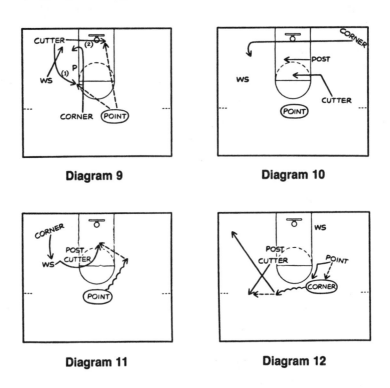

Diagram 9   Diagram 10

Diagram 11   Diagram 12

With this movement the side now will be cleared for the point to drive or shoot. At the same time the post and cutter are clearing out, they are to pick for the weak side who comes off their double screen. If the clear out man can't get the shot off from his drive, he looks for his option, the weak side.

NOTE: Diagram 11 shows the option for clear out man if shot is not taken from the drive.

If the option won't work, the ball is released to corner man, who has made a complete swing. The corner man must go to the ball. He then balances and goes into the pattern on the left side.

NOTE: Diagram 12 shows release, movement and reset into pattern on the left side.

Conclusion

With different series, interchanges and movement of any man but the post can be put into the clear out position. The above two clear outs have been good situation plays for us in the past years along with our shuffle offense.

9

The One-On-One with Patterns

by Eric Geldart

Head Basketball Coach
Western New England College
Springfield, Massachusetts

Eric Geldart began his twelfth year of coaching in 1973-74. He coached four years of high school, and began his seventh season in the Superior Basketball League in Puerto Rico, and his eighth season at Western New England College (Springfield, Massachusetts). He has coached Puerto Rican teams in international competition, and given clinics in many countries. He holds an island championship in Puerto Rico and a Coach-of-the-Year award with an overall record of 111-62. His seven-year record at Western New England College is 99-62, with two NAIA regional championships and two Coach-of-the-Year awards.

Should you have a group of one-on-one players and feel you want to take advantage of their individual efforts, you might consider the offense we use.

NOTE: Over the past few years, we were faced with out-standing one-on-one players. We arrived at this offense because it requires only one guard, which enables one to

get more height in the game; it cuts down the number of people handling the ball; it has continuity; it gives good defensive balance; and there is constant movement without the ball, which moves the defense.

We feel that you must utilize one-on-one talents, but everyone must operate within a system in order to be successful. Your guard must be a good ball handler and willing to make your offense go by getting the ball up front.

Basic Set-Up

The basic set-up is shown in Diagram 1. #1 is the floor general. As for 2, 3, 4 and 5, the coach must evaluate these players and place them where he thinks they will be most effective.

NOTE: I place my players as shown in Diagram 2.

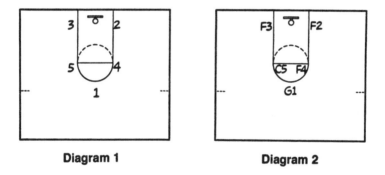

| Diagram 1 | Diagram 2 |

The offense consists of three series with many options in each series. Keep in mind how often the one-on-one situation occurs. Notice how we always arrive back with the same movement. You must teach your players how to set screens, taking advantage of the defensive man's body position as the screen is set.

Series One

Simultaneously, O5 and O4 go down to set screens for O3 and O2, as O3 and O2 brush the outside shoulder of the screen and move to the foul line extended (Diagram 3). Already, everyone on offense knows which man is getting the ball because O1 started the offense to the right side of the imaginary line with which we divide the floor.

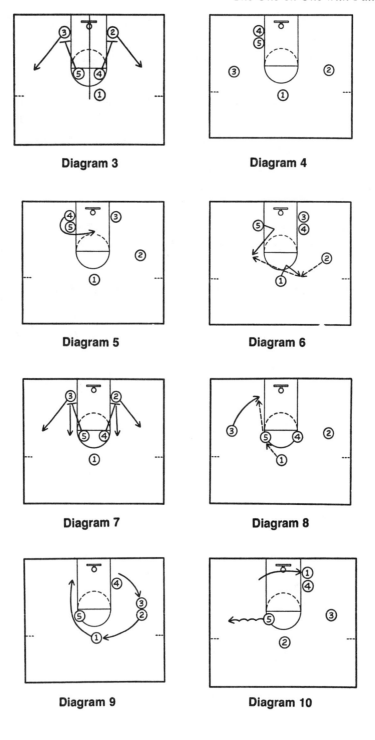

Diagram 3   Diagram 4

Diagram 5   Diagram 6

Diagram 7   Diagram 8

Diagram 9   Diagram 10

NOTE: In this case, O1 will pass to O2 as O4 goes across the lane to set a double screen with O5 who remained after setting the screen for O3. We are now as shown in Diagram 4.

O2 looks to go one-on-one as O3 thinks about defensive balance. When O2 cannot beat his man, O3 cuts off the double screen looking for the layup. As soon as he goes by the screen, O4 cuts to the ball by going around O5. Should O3 receive the ball and shoot, we have good rebounding position (Diagram 5).

If neither O3 nor O4 receives a pass from O2, they form the double screen opposite from where they started; O2 reverses ball to O1, who passes to O5, and we begin cutting over again (Diagram 6). O5 looks to go one-on-one or pass to O2 as he cuts off double screen; thus the offense has continuity.

Series Rules

The rules in this series are:

    A. O1 must be in offensive position on either side of imaginary line before O4 and O5 move.

    B. O4 or O5 clears to opposite side if ball comes to forward on his side. O4 or O5 stays if ball is passed opposite him.

    C. O2 and O3 must wait behind double screen until they see the one-on-one will not work. If O2 shoots, O3 is defensive balance; and if O3 shoots, O2 is defensive balance.

Series Two

From the same alignment O5 and O4 go down and pick for O3 and O2 as O3 and O2 move foul line extended. O5 and O4 return hard to their original positions (Diagram 7) because O1 may pass to anyone.

NOTE: If he passes to O5 or O4, we are looking for the back door or inside cut by O2 or O3 (Diagram 8).

Once O4 sees the ball passed to O5, O4 returns to medium-low post (second foul shot spot) because if O3 does not get pass from O5, O3 will go to the opposite side foul line extended as O1 cuts off O5 for ball, and O2 replaces O1 (Diagram 9).

Let us assume O5 does not give it to O1; O1 continues on through to set double screen with O4 as O5 plays one-on-one or dribbles out to side (Diagram 10). We are now ready to start our cuts off the double screen.

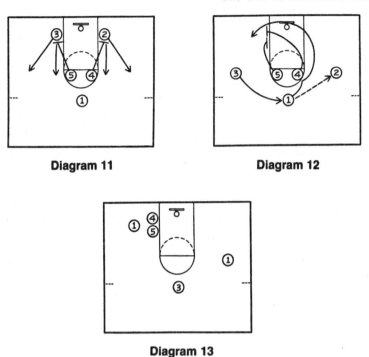

Diagram 11   **Diagram 12**

Diagram 13

**NOTE: Should 01 pass the ball to 02 or 03 at the begin-
ning of the series, we carry through as shown in Diagrams
11, 12 and 13.**

Conclusion

I have briefly covered two of the three series that we run. As you can
see, they offer one-on-one basketball as well as organization. We are
operating in a high-percentage shooting area at all times. Should you ever
try this offense, I would like to hear how it works out.

10

The Controlled Fast Break

by Phil Hora

Head Basketball Coach
Stockbridge High School
Stockbridge, Michigan

*Phil Hora has been head basketball coach at Stockbridge
High School for the past five years. His record there is 83 wins
against 20 losses for an 81% winning record. The best two
seasons have been: 22-1 (1969-70); 32-1 (1970-71). In 1970
his squad lost only in the state semi-finals and in 1971 only in
the state finals. Coach Hora was named Coach-of-the-Year
last season by the Detroit News.*

The fast break is the quickest and easiest way of scoring in basketball,
if it is well organized. We try to discipline our ballplayers to use the fast
break at every opportunity that gives us the advantage over the opposition. We control the fast break by training our ballplayers to stop and set
up every time we do not have the opposition outnumbered.

**NOTE: We work to get a 3-on-2, 2-on-1, or 1-on-0 advan-
tage whenever possible. If we do not have at least this
advantage or an open lane to the basket, we will stop and
run our offense.**

We also believe that a 10- or 15-foot jump shot is not what we are looking for off our fast break, so we discourage this type of shot. We feel we can use our offense to get a better shot. Many times on a fast break our best rebounders are out of good rebounding position. If we should miss the jump shot, we could turn the ball over to the opposition.

Basic Situations

Basketball is a game of strategic situations and we feel the following are the basic situations that are keys to beginning the fast break. Whenever one of these situations occurs, our boys are taught to go into the fast break:

1. The defensive rebound begins our fast break at least 50% of the time, especially against a good ball-handling team. Because the defensive board is so important, we use a lot of rebounding drills and drills that incoporate rebounding, outlet areas, and filling the proper lanes. These drills will be discussed later.

2. The second most important situation for beginning our fast break is the interception. This situation can occur off one of our basic defenses or off one of our presses. If we have the personnel to press effectively, we know we can also fast break, since speed and quickness are necessary for either of these to be successful.

3. Any loose ball situation is an opportunity to fast break. Whenever we are reacting as quickly as we should, we will gain an advantage over the opposition and turn loose balls into fast-break opportunities.

4. We use a couple of jump-ball plays to give us fast-break opportunities. This will only work if you have a size or jumping advantage over the opposition. We have a 6'8" center who jumps well. Consequently, we spend time each week on our fast-break patterns off the jump ball.

5. It is possible to fast break after a basket or free throw, but it is hard to outnumber the opposition so we consider this a secondary fast-break situation. The only time we use this method is late in the game if the opposition is getting tired or is overloading on some type of press.

> **NOTE: In order to make our fast break work, we must condition our ballplayers to react to any of these strategic situations and to adjust from defense to offense quicker than the opposition adjusts. We use three basic defenses and two basic presses. Our man-to-man defense and our 2-1-2 zone defense are basically the same defensive setup. Whenever we use either of these defenses, we have a standard fast-break pattern that we try to run with a few alternatives for unusual situations.**

Basic Setup

Diagram 1 shows our basic setup in either of these defenses. In Diagram 1, X5 rebounds on his side. As soon as it is obvious X5 is going to control the ball, the other four ballplayers must be moving. X2 flares to his side about seven feet from the out-of-bounds line and just above the free-throw line extended. He is ready to receive pass from X5. X1 cuts for mid-court area to receive pass from X2. He is ready to receive ball before he reaches mid-court line. X4 sprints down side opposite rebound to become side man of 3-on-2 break. X3 sprints toward side of rebound whenever forward rebounds.

Filling the Lanes

Diagram 2 shows how the lanes are filled and how we get the ball to the mid-court area with short snappy passes. X5 has fired the ball to guard X2. We like the rebounders to keep the ball over their head, never bringing it down, then turn to the outside to stay out of the congested middle.

X5 always looks to guard X2 and should hit him with the pass. X5, being the rebounder, follows the play down court not going past the 10-second line, so we have one man back on defense in case of a turnover. As soon as he receives the ball X2 hits X1 with a quick pass. X4, X3 and X1 sprint down court in the 3-lane pattern.

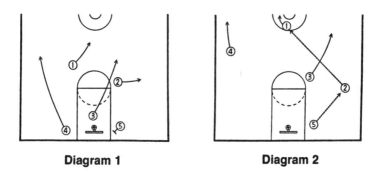

Diagram 1   **Diagram 2**

Pattern in the Front Court

Diagram 3 shows our pattern in the front court. After receiving the pass, X1 has dribbled down the middle until a defensive man stops him. If he is challenged, he may hit the side men at any time, but we try to keep the ball in the middle.

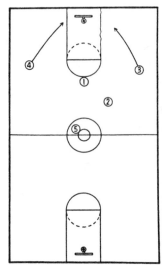

Diagram 3

X1 will stop at the free-throw line unless he has an open lane to the basket. If he stops, he hits X4 or X3 going hard to the basket. X2 is the trailer following the play by 10 to 15 feet. If X4 and X3 are covered, and X1 has stopped, X2 goes hard to the basket and X1 should hit him.

> **NOTE: Many times the defense will have you bottled up and will relax in this situation. The delayed trailer may catch them off guard and give you an easy shot. Of course, if none of these options work, or if we are outnumbered, we stop and set up our offense and work for the good shot.**

Rebounding Triangle

When we are using our 1-3-1 zone, we use basically the same setup pattern for our fast break as we do from our man-to-man or 2-1-2 zone defense. In Diagram 4 we show our rebounding triangle in our 1-3-1 zone which is essential no matter what defense we are using.

In Diagram 5, X5 rebounds and hits X2 with a quick pass. X2 hits X1, the middle man, and X4 takes the other side which gives us our same fast-break pattern. X3 or X2 will take the right side. The one who gets there first takes that side and the other man becomes the trailer.

In Diagram 6 the same offensive man shoots, but the rebound goes to the weak side. X4 rebounds and X1 must come to this side to get a quick pass. X2 becomes the middle man and X5 takes the other side in the

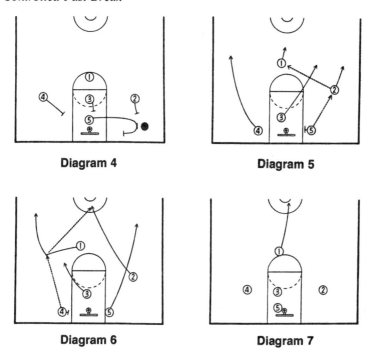

Diagram 4   Diagram 5

Diagram 6   Diagram 7

three-man break. X3 is the trailer and X4, the rebounder, stays at the 10-second line on defense.

Release Fast-Break Option

When we find a team that has its guards going to the basket, we have a release fast-break option that has been very successful for us. Diagram 7 illustrates this situation. As soon as the offense shoots, defensive guard X1 releases and sprints down the floor. It makes no difference which man rebounds, because as soon as he has control of the ball he wheels around and throws a long baseball pass to X1 streaking toward the opponent's basket.

> **NOTE: This fast-break option will not work on every rebound, but it has worked in a lot of our games. When it does work, it is very demoralizing to a team that has worked hard to get a good shot off their offense. Our release play looks so much easier and quicker.**

Our release play also will keep many opponents' guards from going to the basket because they are trying to stop us from getting the easy basket.

Consequently, their offense will not be as effective if their guards are not in the right place in their pattern offense. We can also release the weak-side guard out of our 2-1-2 zone as soon as an offensive player has shot. It can be just as effective as when we are releasing from our 1-3-1 zone.

Fast Break Off Diamond Press

When we are pressing or on any interception we are also very conscious of our fast-break possibilities. We usually press with a diamond-and-one or with a man-to-man. In either situation, we have at least as many men in scoring position as the opposition. Diagram 8 shows an example of our fast break off our diamond press.

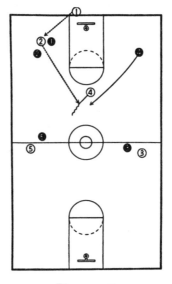

Diagram 8

X1 and X2 are double-teaming the offensive man after he has received an inbounds pass. If X4 or X5 intercepts the pass, we have them outnumbered at least 3-on-2 or 4-on-3 because a defensive man will be between the ball and the man he is guarding. If X1 or X2 stops the pass or takes the ball away from the offensive man, we will still have them 3-on-2 or 3-on-1.

> **NOTE: As long as our defensive men are reacting quickly on all turnovers, and are always conscious of our quick-basket possibilities, we will keep having success getting the easy basket.**

Jump-Ball Situations

Since we have a 6'8" jumping center, we almost always control jump-ball situations when he is the jumper. We like to fast break in this situation when possible. We have three basic patterns to accomplish this. One of the most successful is shown in Diagram 9.

Our center tips the ball to O4, our tall forward. As soon as the referee puts the ball up, O1 breaks down side and O5 sprints down his side. O4 becomes the middle man of the fast break and usually we will have a 3-on-2 situation. O3 becomes the trailer and O2 stays back on defense.

NOTE: The only way they can stop this is by putting three men in our forecourt and conceding the jump ball to us.

 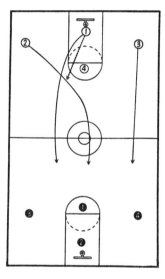

Diagram 9   **Diagram 10**

We also have a couple of options off this center jump play, but basically they are all similar and will all work unless our opponents are stacking their back-court to stop our fast break.

Conditioning and Drills

Conditioning is what makes our fast-break offense as effective as it has been. Our basic philosophy when it comes to drills is—run, run, run. Along with the running we spend a lot of time on ball handling, passing at full speed, and reacting to fast-break possibilities and situations encountered when fast breaking.

NOTE: I feel wind sprints are very beneficial to building speed and endurance. During pre-season practice, we run sprints before and after practice. We start off with 15 to 20 sprints and finish practice with a minimum of 20 sprints. When we get into our regular season we do not run sprints before practice, but we do them after practice with the exception of the night before a game.

We use the full-court 3-man weave drill and the 5-man weave drill quite often because it is a very good conditioner and a good drill for working on passing at full speed. Another favorite is the shot-gun fast-break drill. This continuous drill is shown in Diagram 10.

EXECUTION: O1 starts the drill by rebounding off the board. O1 hits O2 going to the middle. O3 takes one side and O1 sprints to the other size. Now it is a 3-on-2 drill with ●1 and ●2 being the defense. After the offense has scored or missed, ●2 retrieves the ball and hits ●4 going to the middle and the drill continues in the same manner. ●1 moves to the back defense spot and O2 becomes the front defensive man so the drill can continue uninterrupted.

We use the half-court 3-on-2 and 2-on-1 drills quite often in practice to teach the boys the possibilities of passing and easy scoring in these fast-break situations. We also spend considerable time on 5-man fast-break patterns after getting the defensive rebound. We run this drill without defense sometimes, but we will also run it against a 2-man or 3-man defensive unit.

Conclusion

You must sell your ballplayers on the fast break in order for it to work properly. One loafer can kill the fast-break offense and if you have such a player, he must be replaced. If your opponents do not want to run, you can still set the game tempo by running on offense and using ball-hawking defensive tactics.

If necessary, a press can speed the tempo and make the game your type of running game. I feel the fast break may cost a ball team a few more turnovers than they would have without running—but at the same time a good fast break will get enough easy baskets to more than make up for the turnovers.

11

The One-Three-One Free-Lance Offense

by Sam J. Andy

Head Basketball Coach
Wheeling High School
Wheeling, West Virginia

Sam J. Andy has been coaching high school basketball for the past ten years–the last four as head basketball coach at Wheeling High School. His record there is 69-24 and includes three sectional championships, two regional championships, three city championships, and three Mountaineer League championships. His 1970-71 and 1972-73 squads ranked third in the state. Coach Andy's overall record is 144-53.

The 1-3-1 free-lance offense has proven to be a very effective one during my two seasons at Wheeling High School. We averaged 89.5 points per game and shot 43.6 percent for the 1969-70 season and 94.5 points per game and 46.5 percent for the 1970-71 season.

> **NOTE: We feel that this high scoring average and high shooting percentage are due to our getting the shot in the high-percentage areas of the court.**

Shooting Drills

We emphasize area shooting from the high-percentage area in our practice sessions by spending a great deal of time on shooting drills. Our point man will take 75 to 100 shots per day from his area at the top right and left of the key hole. Our wing men will take the same amount of shots from their area and our high-post men will shoot from the foul line, with the corner men shooting out of both corners.

We make these drills as competitive as possible by always using a defensive man on the shooter and by having a third man passing the ball to the shooter. You do not accomplish very much unless your shooter is always moving to get the ball and always shooting with defensive pressure. We also keep statistics on our practice shooting.

> **NOTE: Diagrams 1, 2, 3 and 4 illustrate our shooting drills for the point men, wing men, post men and corner men. In these diagrams 1 is the passer; 2 the shooter; 3 the defensive man.**

Pressure Lay-Ups

We also shoot 100 lay-ups every day in practice and all of these are shot against a defensive man who is permitted to bump and hit the shooter. We feel that the lay-up must be practiced against defensive pressure at all times.

> **NOTE: Our pressure lay-ups are illustrated in Diagrams 5, 6 and 7. Diagram 5 shows 1 driving for the basket with 2 coming across for defensive pressure; Diagram 6 shows 1 driving with 2 coming from an angle to apply pressure; Diagram 7 shows 1 driving with 2 chasing from behind.**

Our favorite group shooting drill is to divide the squad into two groups of six with the winner being the first group to make 30 baskets from a designated area of the floor. The losers run an extra sprint at the end of practice.

Basic Man-To-Man Offense

We have discussed our shooting drills before getting into our offense because we feel that you must work on your shooting constantly under pressure in order to be a high scoring team. We are a run-and-shoot team with the philosophy that we are going to get 20 to 30 more shots than our opponents and that we are going to shoot 45 percent.

Our offense is designed to be uncomplicated and as simple as possible. Our two basic offensive rules are: (1) Any time you feel you can beat your man to the basket—do it. (2) Any time you feel you have a good shot——take it.

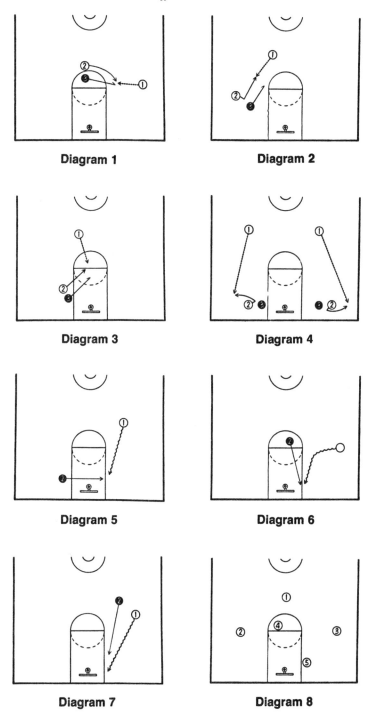

Diagram 1

Diagram 2

Diagram 3

Diagram 4

Diagram 5

Diagram 6

Diagram 7

Diagram 8

NOTE: Diagram 8 shows our basic man-to-man offense alignment. 1 is our quarterback. He must be a good ball handler, good feeder, and must have good range up to 20 feet, with a strong drive. 2 and 3 must have good range, 15 to 20 feet, strong drive and be good rebounders. 4 is our pivot man. He must have good range, 15 feet, good drive, and be strong on the boards, 5 is our roamer. He must have a good corner shot, must be a good feeder and be strong on the boards.

To start the play, 1 passes to 2 with 4 setting a pick for 3 who jab-steps toward the basket and breaks around the pick. 4 con nues down and sets a pick for 5 breaking across low (Diagram 9).

Options

There are many options available from this play once the defense starts anticipating the picks. For instance, 4 starts motion to set his pick and does a reverse pivot toward the basket.

This prevents the defense from making the automatic switch across the middle (Diagram 10). Or 3 will go behind the pick set by 4 with 5 coming across high (Diagram 11).

Another option with this offensive alignment is to catch 1's defensive man sleeping. 4 starts toward 3 and breaks to the top of the key to pick for 1 who takes a jab step left and breaks off the pick by 4. 4 rolls behind 1 with 3 covering for defensive balance (Diagram 12).

Diagram 13 illustrates our isolation play. We are simply trying to play one-on-one basketball because we feel we can beat the opponents in a one-on-one situation.

Two-on-two basketball is shown in Diagram 14. 4 breaks to the low post with 5 breaking up to pick for 3 who comes across high. 2 gets the ball to 3 or 4 and breaks to the basket.

Diagram 15 shows 4 breaking low and picking for 5 who comes across low with 3 breaking the middle high.

Zone Offense

Our zone offensive philosophy is that we can move the ball faster with good sharp passes than the zone defense can react. We spend a lot of practice time moving the ball against the various zone defenses.

NOTE: We like to time our offense's possession against an eight-man zone. We work on not dribbling the ball against

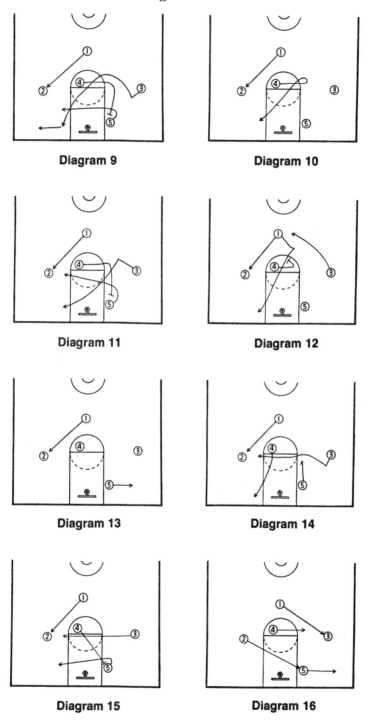

Diagram 9

Diagram 10

Diagram 11

Diagram 12

Diagram 13

Diagram 14

Diagram 15

Diagram 16

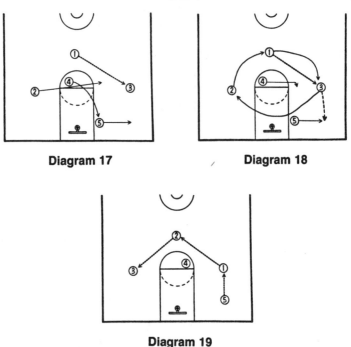

Diagram 17   /   Diagram 18

Diagram 19

a zone. We feel that the dribble should only be used when absolutely necessary against the zone defense.

As shown in Diagram 16, 1 feeds 3 with 5 going to the corner. 4 comes across high with the backside wing man (2) coming across low.

In Diagram 17, everything is the same as in Diagram 16, with one exception—4 breaks across low and 2 comes across high.

In Diagram 18, 1 feeds 3 who gets the ball to 5 in the corner and goes through to the backside wing with 1 going to the wing and 2 going to the point.

In Diagram 19 the ball is swung around quickly to 3 on the backside for the short jumper.

Conclusion

This offense is uncomplicated and designed to get the shot quickly from the high-percentage areas. The 1-3-1 free lance has been very effective for us—and we feel that it's the best offense for a run-and-shoot team.

12

Beating the Press

by James Deane Houdeshell

Head Basketball Coach
Findlay College
Findlay, Ohio

*Dr. James D. Houdeshell is a professor of physical educa-
tion, athletic director and head basketball coach at Findlay
College. His 18-year basketball record is 256-175. This includes four conference championships, 11 NAIA #22 playoffs,
and three NAIA #22 championships. Coach Houdeshell has
had four All-American choices in the NAIA.*

One of the most frustrating things to witness on a basketball court is a
team wilting before the press. For some time, we felt its humiliation, too.
However, we have had some success with the pattern to be discussed in
this article.

**NOTE: In preparing a team to use this offense we must
instill confidence in what we are teaching. To do this, we
work against several pressing styles. Also, we work on it
often as the players soon realize it can give them an occasional fast break.**

Position of Players

We position our players according to the abilities we want in each
position. Diagram 1 shows the positions assumed on the court. Players 4

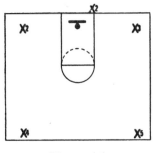

Diagram 1

and 5 are our biggest. They are looking for the pass-in while moving to their position.

The out-of-bounds man (1), a good passer, must look first to the breaking men and should throw the ball high and to the outside shoulder of either. As he has only five seconds, he must decide quickly.

> **NOTE: We stress the quick pass-in as we have had several fast breaks result from this pattern.**

Our two back-court corner men are our quickest ball handlers, and they must fake and move to free themselves for the pass-in. They must, if the pass is up-court, be ready to move into the pattern quickly.

We have our out-of-bounds man and the two back-court men work in all three spots so we can interchange the men if necessary. To habituate players in what to do is one of our major goals.

> **NOTE: This pattern results from any defense because we instruct one person to take the out-of-bounds pass-in position.**

First Option

Our two biggest men break for the sidelines at the 10-second line. Both look for the pass-in. If it is made to one, he proceeds, if open, to bring the ball across the 10-second line. The other breaks for the basket and if open receives the pass. We call this our first option and it is shown in Diagrams 2 and 3.

Second Option

If he cannot make this first pass, he holds up the ball for the back-court men, or if open, he will drive on the basket himself.

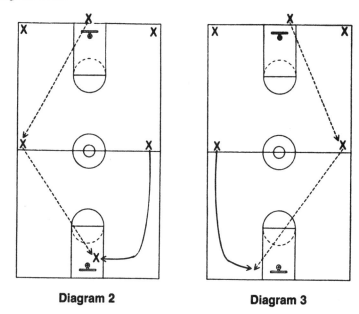

Diagram 2   **Diagram 3**

An occasional opportunity for a 3-on-2 or 3-on-1 fast break results from this first pass as the opposite back-court corner man comes to the middle of the court. This is shown in Diagrams 4 and 5 and is what we call our second option.

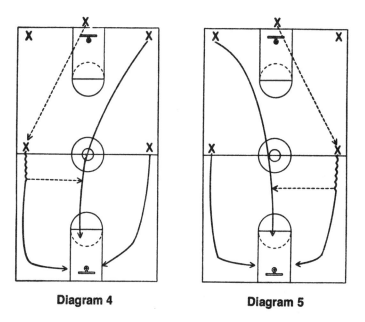

Diagram 4   **Diagram 5**

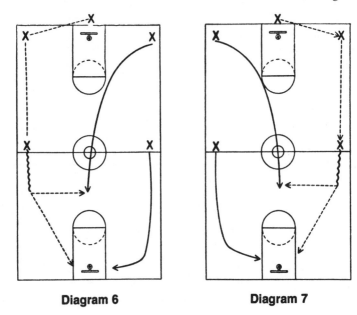

Diagram 6   **Diagram 7**

Hit the Big Man

The out-of-bounds player, if he cannot make the first pass option, will look to the back-court corner men. After this pass-in, the corner man has as his option to hit the big man to his side. If this can be done, we attempt to follow the pattern of our first option. Diagrams 6 and 7 show this.

Pass to Opposite Corner Man

The second option for the corner man is to pass to the opposite corner man as he cuts to the middle. This gives us again an opportunity to beat the press with the 3-on-2 or 3-on-1 fast break.

NOTE: This depends on the type of press. After the middle man receives the ball, he continues until stopped, working to gain the restriction line. (See Diagrams 8 and 9.)

Third Option

The third option for the back-court corner man is to return the ball to the out-of-bounds man, who has cut toward the vacated corner.

NOTE: He then brings the ball up while the breaking men force the defense to cover them up-court. (See Diagrams 10 and 11.)

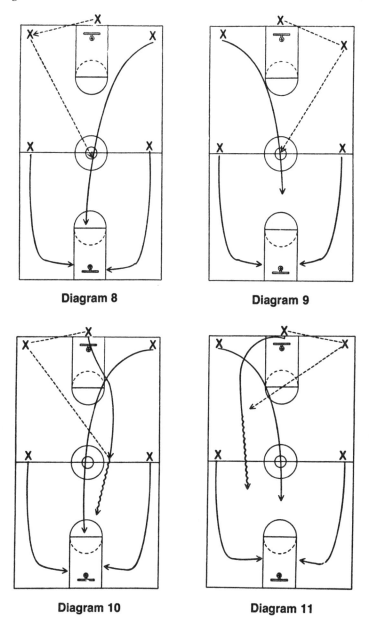

Diagram 8   **Diagram 9**

Diagram 10   **Diagram 11**

Last Move

As a last resort, the back-court corner man will bring the ball up himself, as the pressure exerted on the defense by the up-court rush will almost surely leave him open or one-on-one.

NOTE: This is our pattern if the opponent plans a man-to-man no-switch.

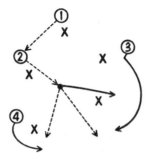

Diagram 12

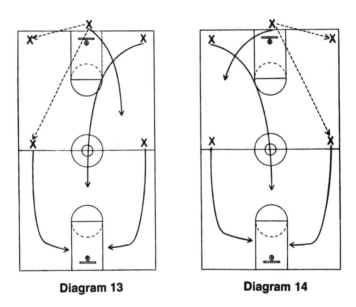

Diagram 13   **Diagram 14**

Adjustment

An adjustment made to handle some of the zone pressures is for the better of our two big men (4 and 5) to cut to the center of the back court. He becomes the pass outlet for the corner man. The adjustment is shown in Diagram 12. The overall pattern of the men on the rush up-court is shown in Diagrams 13 and 14.

Conclusion

A coaching point that we stress is to use the width of the floor. Realizing that there are many press defenses, we strive to teach the options and to make adjustments within the pattern shown.

13

The Offensive Pass Key

by D. Bruce MacGregor

Head Basketball Coach
Husson College
Bangor, Maine

During Bruce MacGregor's five years as Husson College's basketball coach, he has led the Braves to a 79-33 record.

In 1970 he coached the Braves to 22 wins with only three losses. For his effort, MacGregor received three separate coaching awards, including being named New England Small College Coach-of-the-Year by United Press International, and being selected as Maine's College Athletics Coach-of-the-Year for District 32 (New England).

Prior to joining the Husson staff, Coach MacGregor coached at Reading Memorial High School in Massachusetts where his team compiled a record of 90-20. In 11 years of college and high school coaching, his teams have won 169 games out of 222 for a 76% win record.

Basketball was devised to be a quick game. Recent changes not only have sped up the game but have made it one of continual movement. The more a team deviates from this constant movement the less effective it becomes as an offense.

NOTE: Any type of break in play movement allows the opponent needed time to defense a play. To insure offen-

sive movement, many teams have inserted visual or auditory keys to initiate offensive patterns.

Visual vs. Auditory

With the advent of the pressure defense, it became difficult for an
offensive team to key by visual signs. The guard has enough difficulty
advancing the ball up-court against pressure defense without raising an
arm to indicate with his fingers if a one, two or three play is to be started.

**NOTE: It seems incredible that we would ask a guard
closely guarded to forget the protection of the ball in order
to start the offense.**

The boisterous crowd has made auditory keys difficult if not impossible
to use during a big game. Many teams have found that the auditory keys
that worked so well in practice have been disastrous during a game.

Offensive Desires

Most coaches want their teams to run offensive patterns. And most
coaches also want more than one offensive option and/or offensive continuity. To achieve these it is necessary to have some form of offensive
key. The key to be used must be easily recognized by all five members of
the offensive team. Once the key is given all five men must swing into the
offensive pattern.

**PASS KEY: To eliminate the problems suggested by the
auditory or visual keys and to give the offensive keys
needed to run an effective offense, I suggest starting the
offense with a pass key.**

Three Basic Keys

Once the offensive team is balanced on the offensive end of the court
the first pass made can easily swing the offense into motion. In this
fashion, the offensive players can initiate their offense according to where
the ball is passed.

**NOTE: Your offense can be as simple or complex as you
want with the pass key. For illustration purposes you have
at least 3 basic keys in a 2-1-2 offense. You have a key from
a guard to guard pass (Diagram 1); from a guard to for-**

ward pass (Diagram 2); from a guard to center pass (Diagram 3).

Offensive Patterns

To further illustrate the three basic pass keys, let's review several offensive patterns which might be run by the right guard.

Guard-to-guard pass key: This key might start a four-man weave with outside hand-offs. See Diagrams 4 and 5.

Guard-to-forward pass key: This pass sets up the second offensive option. This option might be the team's main offensive play with its continuity. See Diagrams 6 through 11.

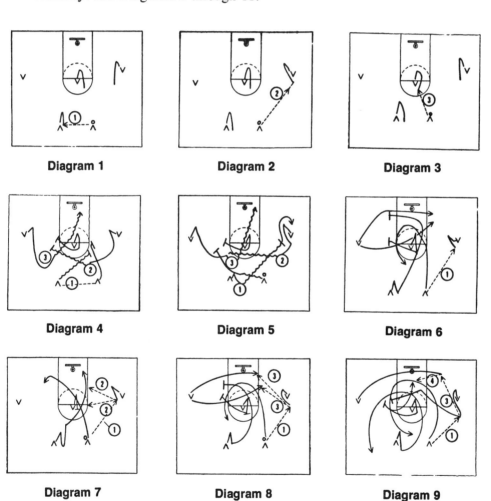

Diagram 1   Diagram 2   Diagram 3

Diagram 4   Diagram 5   Diagram 6

Diagram 7   Diagram 8   Diagram 9

NOTE: With men returning to the original 2-1-2 formation the play can continue or a pass key can start a different patt rn.

Guard-to-center pass key: By adding the backdoor cut to the three passing keys a new scoring threat is added. If we are going to use the backdoor cut we have the guard fake a two-handed pass to his teammate or "show him the ball"—this indicates he wants the backdoor cut. See Diagrams 12 and 13.

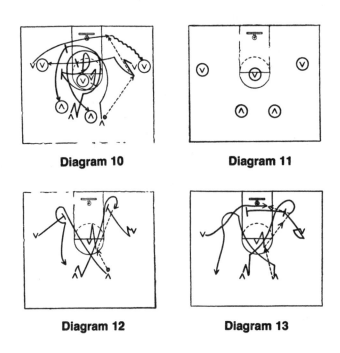

Diagram 10   Diagram 11

Diagram 12   Diagram 13

Multiple Continuity

It appears, at first glance, that this would be a complicated offense to run, but in reality you are running only three plays—a weave; a modified scissors off the center; and your continuity.

I am sure that many coaches have three offensive plays. With the pass key you really add another dimension. You have a multiple continuity which appears more complicated than it is. It makes your team more difficult to scout or defense since you can change after one pattern and go into the next without a visual or auditory key.

Advantages of the Pass Key

1. Each man without the ball will work to get free so he can start the offense.
2. Crowd noise will not hinder the pass key.
3. Pressure defense will not hinder the pass key.
4. The player with the ball hits the open man to start the offense. The man with the ball is not forced to pass.
5. A new dimension is given to the offense with a multiple continuity which appears more complicated than it is.
6. The pass key makes your team more difficult to scout because there isn't a visual or auditory key or break in movement.
7. It makes your team more difficult to defense, since there are different patterns for each pass. Consequently, your opponent has more to think about in defending your team.
8. All your players are involved. This makes for a happier ball club.
9. The offense is not left up to *one* player; consequently each man is dependent on all the others to get the ball.
10. Your team has good floor balance on each play and at the conclusion of each play.
11. Confidence is instilled, for with the first pass each player makes a move he has practiced numerous times. Players know which shots they will be getting in a game.
12. If the fast break is thwarted the offense can be quickly started.
13. *Most important*, continual movement is maintained.

Part II

Defensive Play

1

The Match-Up Zone Defense

by Cal Luther

Head Basketball Coach
Murray State University
Murray, Kentucky

Since coming to Murray State University as head coach in 1958, Cal Luther's teams have won 231 games and lost 139. In the Ohio Valley Conference, where every game is a life or death affair, they have won 124 games and lost 84. Coach Luther has had 14 straight winning seasons. His teams have won three conference championships and one tournament championship. In six of the past seven seasons, his teams have either won the Ohio Valley Conference championship or have been the runner-up. His 1964 and 1969 teams represented the Ohio Valley Conference in the NCAA Tournament.

For several years at Murray State we have employed a zone defense in which we "match-up" on the zone offensive attack of our opponents.

BEST ATTRIBUTES: This defense enables us to combine the best attributes of both the zone and man-to-man defense, as well as its being a very confusing defense for our opponents to play against.

When playing opponents on whom we have complete scouting information, including their basic zone offense, we can usually use our ''match-up'' technique very successfully. Here's how it works.

Basic zone alignment: This technique against a known zone offensive pattern attempts to overplay the zone pattern attack and match-up on the personnel, choking off the cutting and passing lanes as much as possible. In this defense we set up basically in a 2-1-2 zone alignment (Diagram 1).

> **NOTE: If our opponent uses a ''2-out set'' to initiate their zone attack, we are in good position to ''match-up''—however, if our opponent uses a ''1-out set,'' it is necessary to slide one of our front two zone men to a wing position.**

We accomplish this by rotating our 2-1-2 zone counter-clockwise causing it to convert to a 1-3-1 zone alignment (Diagram 2).

Match-up technique: One of the most common offensive techniques against the zone is to pass to the base line man from the wing and send the wingman through the defense to the weak side. Our ''match-up'' handles this technique as illustrated in Diagram 3.

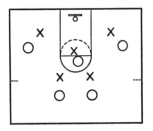

Diagram 1

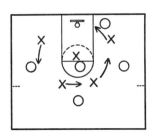

Diagram 2

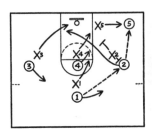

Diagram 3

Defensive wing man: The defensive wing man (X2) plays the offensive man aggressively and attempts to ''choke off'' his cut through the defense as much as possible. He will cover the wing man for two or three steps into the defense, then release him and ''match-up'' on the next offensive player moving into this area.

> **NOTE: If no offensive player moves into this immediate area, he ''matches-up'' on the next man to his right toward the middle of the defense.**

Baseline defensive man: The baseline defensive man (X5) matches up on the offensive baseline man as soon as the pass is made. He plays this man aggressively and protects against the baseline drive.

Middle defensive man: The middle defensive man (X4) matches up on anyone in the pivot post area from the free-throw line to the base line area. If there is no one in this immediate area initially, he zones between the ball and the goal, and "matches-up" on the first offensive player to cut into this area.

Point defensive man: The point defensive man (X1) will match up on the point offensive man; when the ball moves to the wings or the baseline area he will drop to the middle of the defense and play to the side of the ball. If his opponent, the opposing point man, remains fairly stationary (as some teams will play this man against the zone), (X1) has few problems matching up with this man.

> NOTE: However, if this man rotates to or away from the ball, the point man (X1) will match up on the next offensive player coming into his zone area, or the first offensive player to his right from the free-throw line extending out.

Defensive wing man: The defensive wing man (X3) matches up on his offensive wing man initially, and when the ball penetrates the defense opposite his position, he drops to the weak side goal area where he has the

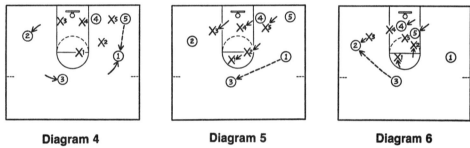

| Diagram 4 | Diagram 5 | Diagram 6 |

assignment of covering the important weak side rebounding area. Against the zone defense described, he will pick up the offensive wing man cutting through the defense and match up on him if the ball is successful in getting around the defense back to the weak side.

> NOTE: Our match-up technique as the ball moves around the perimeter of the defense is illustrated in Diagrams 4, 5, and 6.

Change-up: As a change-up to this combination defense, we will sometimes start out in our basic zone, rotate to our "match up" positions, and then on a verbal call, change to a strict switching, man-to-man defense in which we attempt to play the ball aggressively, switch all cross and cutter situations, and sluff our defense inside as much as possible. We can many times convert to this defense for long periods of time without our opponent recognizing we have changed completely to a switching man-to-man defense.

> **NOTE: One technique that must be mastered and recognized by your team in attempting to play this type of defense is that whenever the offensive team becomes confused and attempts to become reorganized by taking the ball back on the floor deep and realigning their personnel, the defensive team must recognize this readjustment and convert immediately to their original "zone-set" and then begin their "match up" sequence again as the ball begins to move.**

Usually the offensive team will help you in making this adjustment by becoming very deliberate in trying to place their personnel. Many times they will call out "zone defense, let's set up." We have used a verbal sign to alert our defense to convert to our original "match up" zone in these instances, so that we will allow the first cutter to go free and then rotate into our "match up" situations.

Variations: There are some interesting variations that can be easily employed when using this combination defense—and it all adds to the problem that the offense must combat in facing this type of defensive deployment. It takes a poised and experienced team to successfully combat through an entire game a good match-up zone and combination defense. You may want to consider adding this defensive combination to your repertoire of defensive stunts.

2

Coaching the 1-2-2 Ball Press

by Ron Ferguson

Head Basketball Coach
Thornridge High School
Dolton, Illinois

A graduate of the University of Illinois, Ron Ferguson coached basketball for 17 years. The first five were spent at Thornton of Harvey under the late Tom Nisbet and Bill Purden, present head coach at Valparaiso University. Coach Ferguson took over at Thornridge in 1960 when the school opened, and was head coach for 12 years until retiring two years ago to become athletic director. During that time Thornridge won two consecutive State Championships in 1971 and 1972 with an overall record of 64-1. Included in this record are 54 consecutive wins which is a State of Illinois record. Thornridge was 141-34 during Coach Ferguson's last six years. The undefeated 1972 team, lead by Quinn Buckner, Boyd Batts, and Mike Bonczyk, was the top prep team in the nation that year, and is rated the best ever to represent the State of Illinois. For these accomplishments Coach Ferguson was named Illinois Coach-of-the-Year for two consecutive years, District 2 National Coach-of-the-Year in 1972, and was named to the Illinois Basketball Hall of Fame in 1972. Coach Ferguson still serves as Vice-President of the Illinois Basketball Coaches Association and appears on numerous basketball clinics through-out the United States.

After several years of experimenting with several types of zone press-es, we have found that the 1-2-2 ball press is the one that best suits our needs.

NOTE: Our personnel have average height (positions on the 1-2-2 ball press are interchangeable and offensive re-bounding is not critical); plus, our boys rarely have excep-tional speed and quickness.

The ball press has been our basic defense for the past three years. While the majority of the ideas for the 1-2-2 ball press come from Coach Virgil Fletcher (Collinsville, Illinois, High School), some of the pressing philosophies and ideas of John Wooden (U.C.L.A.) have also been in-corporated into our pressing defense.

Why Use the Press?

Advantages: There are many advantages in using a press all of the time. The reason we use a three-quarter court press is because you have more time to set up after a missed basket than you would with a full-court press, and it is harder for the opponents to get organized offensively than it would be against a half-court press. The ten-second rule becomes more of a factor.

NOTE: Other advantages are: it forces opponents out of their normal style of offensive play; it makes it hard for the opponent to recreate your defens uring their practice; it saves your defense from making .anges week-to-week; it makes the offense sustain action; it forces opponents to hurry and make errors; also, pressing is great for team spirit—kids like to press.

The principal value lies in demoralizing the opposition. Often times, coaches become upset and scream at players—players then become angry and tend to blame each other for bad passes and mistakes.

Disadvantages: Of course, the ball press has its disadvantages—it becomes necessary at times to sacrifice some offensive rebounding against fast-breaking teams in order to get the defense organized; it might create excessive fouling (however, if you don't reach in, many fouls will be eliminated); it doesn't always take advantage of the big man who is good defensively around the basket.

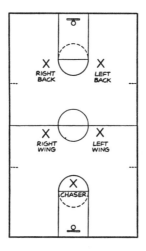

Diagram 1

Positions and Characteristics of Personnel

The positions and characteristics of personnel in the press are as follows: the chaser; right and left wing; right and left back (Diagram 1).

Chaser: Usually the smallest and fastest man on the team; must be in excellent physical condition. He has the least amount of rebounding responsibility but should be good on break-a-way drive-in shot because he will frequently benefit from interception or steal by a teammate.

Wings: Ideally, the smallest forward and the biggest guard should occupy these positions; however, good ball handling on fast-break situations and the ability to score are more important because of the great number of scoring opportunities which arise. The ability to stop a dribbler defensively and some quickness are also important to this position.

Backs: Center and biggest forward usually occupy these positions. Good rebounding and sound defense when at a disadvantage are also important. While quickness will help bring about interceptions-—alertness, position, and unselfishness are of prime importance to the back positions.

Rules for Ball Defense

The only thing that's important is the ball. The following rules are not rigid—they must be flexible.

Chaser: Play the ball all the time except on the basketside of the free-throw line (both ends of the court). At the defensive end of the court cover the middle, or high in lane when ball is beyond the free-throw line. At offensive end of the court play the middle and towards the ball until ball is advanced upcourt by a dribble or pass—then attack.

> **NOTE: Also, drop off approximately five feet when man with ball picks up dribble—cover middle; don't challenge ball on inbounds except when ball is taken out between free-throw lines.**

The chaser must pick up ball quickly after defensive rebound by opponents and delay ball until flankers are in position. Make the offense keep ball in their court as long as possible. Help weakside rebounding and go to weakside board for along rebound. Don't reach for the ball at any time.

Wings: The wing on the ball side will attack when the chaser attacks; the wing on the opposite side from the ball will cover the middle. On a pass thrown overhead—attack from the front and the rear. Have weakside rebounding responsibility when the ball is on the opposite side of the court; cover low (weakside) when ball passes free-throw line extended.

> **NOTE: All passes thrown inside should be attacked front and rear; wings must be interchangeable at times. They must make rapid change from offense to defense. Don't let dribbler go up sideline—force him to the middle where you will have help to stop him. Until chaser attacks, adjust position to cover open men in area—invite to throw long.**

Backs: The backs' main responsibility is intercepting passes and preventing easy baskets. If two offensive men are behind you, do not cover the middle unless sure of interception or deflection. If only one offensive man is behind you or one of the two men behind you breaks up, you may cover the middle aggressively.

> **NOTE: Backs have corner responsibility when the ball is on their side of the floor; strong side rebounder (primary) when the ball is on opposite side of floor; responsible for low post when opposite back is covering outside.**

Special Situations

Rebounding responsibilities and plan: We divide the court into three zones to determine rebounding responsibility (Diagram 2). The various duties depend upon from which zone the ball is shot.

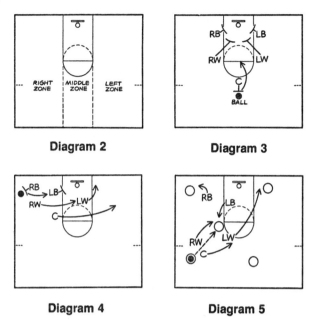

Diagram 2   Diagram 3

Diagram 4   Diagram 5

1. Middle zone: When the ball is shot from the middle zone (Diagram 3), the duties are—chaser covers shooter and long rebound; right and left wing cover middle (where ball is likely to come); right and left back are primary rebounders underneath on their respective sides.

2. Right zone: When ball is shot from right zone (Diagram 4), the duties are—chaser takes the weakside long rebound; very important. Also picks up many deflected balls; left wing is the weakside primary rebounder; right wing has the primary middle responsibility; left back is the strongside primary rebounder; right back covers shooter and long rebound.

3. Left zone: When the ball is shot from the left zone, the responsibilities are just the opposite of those for the right.

Covering middle: Normally the middle is covered by the wing opposite the side of the floor the ball is on when the ball is located between the free-throw lines and—by the chaser when the ball penetrates past the free-throw line. One of the big problems arising is how the middle is covered when the wing is unable to prevent the ball from getting into the middle. We handle this problem in the following manner (Diagram 5).

Left wing. As soon as possible after the ball is thrown to the middle, left wing sprints to cover weakside under basket. He must react quickly—but this is a difficult pass for the offensive man while his back is to the basket.

Left back. Delays slightly before coming up on man with the ball to make sure wing is covering underneath. Better to give jump shot than lay-up. Our back man from side of floor opposite that from which ball was thrown in from must cover middle.

Right back. Covers other forward or offensive player on the ball side of the floor who is the primary outlet. If the right back covers the middle by mistake, it usually will result in an easy lay-up shot.

Right wing. Follows pass into middle and plays man from front and side.

Chaser. Follows pass into middle and keeps offensive man from driving across lane or feeding underneath. Tries to make offensive man throw ball back out or take off-balance shot.

> **NOTE: Assignments, of course, would be just the opposite if the ball were thrown in from the other side of the floor.**

Getting into press after missed shot: One of the strongest points of the 1-2-2 three-quarter court press is the comparative ease with which you can get into it after a missed shot. When the ball is definitely in the possession of the opponents, each player must sprint to his assigned position on the floor and then turn around and play defense.

> **NOTE: The position to which each player sprints is determined by where the ball rebounds or the location on the floor where the opponents gain possession. If the ball were rebounded on the defensive left side, the positions on the floor would look as shown in Diagram 6.**

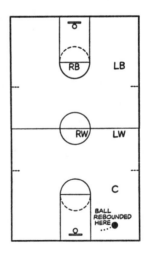

Diagram 6

Chaser checks for sleeper down court and then picks up ball and delays as long as possible to give men time to set up.

Left wing sprints to center line at left side of the court and picks up the ball.

Right wing sprints to center line at middle of court and covers middle.

Left back sprints to free-throw line extended on left side of court and plays defense.

Right back sprints to free-throw line in middle of the court and plays defense.

> **NOTE: If the ball is rebounded to the defensive right, the assignments are the opposite. If the ball is rebounded straight out in frot of the basket, both wings sprint to the center circle and turn around and adjust to whatever direction the chaser has turned the ball. The backs do the same from the free-throw line.**

Fast break from steal or interception: Whenever we steal the ball or intercept a pass, we try to score. Our chaser is always breaking towards the basket on any turnover. If he doesn't get the ball, he always comes back out on the weak side. The wing on the side of the interception breaks down the sideline on the same side as the ball. The wing covering the middle tries to get open in the middle for a pass or, if he doesn't get the ball, cuts hard down the middle. The other man not involved (usually a back man) comes down the weak side.

> **NOTE: When the center intercepts, he usually has a direct line to the basket. When a wing intercepts, the above assignments will still hold true. Until we made these assignments, we often had the problem of too many men breaking directly for the basket and fighting each other for the ball.**

Drills for the Press

Any good defensive drills, of course, will benefit the pressing defense. Here are some we use almost every day which we feel best express the principles of the press.

Two-on-one: We put two defensive players on one offensive player (Diagram 7) and require the defensive players to stop the dribbler before mid-court or face a designated penalty. We stress not reaching in—and use of the legs. Eventually, we require the defenders to put their hands

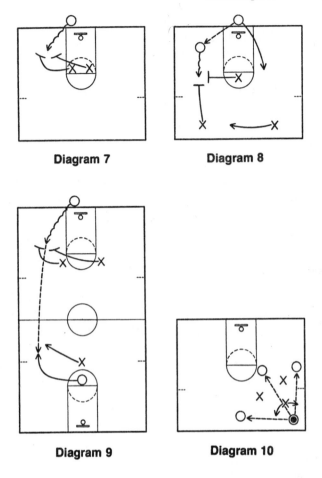

Diagram 7   **Diagram 8**

Diagram 9   **Diagram 10**

behind their back or hold a towel around their neck so that they forget their hands.

Three-on-two: Two offensive players try to bring the ball up the floor against three defensive players (Diagram 8). Offensive players cannot cross center line until the ball does.

Two-on-one with a back: On this drill (Diagram 9), we try to get some work for our back men against the long lob pass. The dribbler can pass the ball down the floor any time—but the man down the floor must stay in the front court.

> **NOTE: If the dribbler gets by the defense, then the back man plays two-on-one defense.**

Reaction passing: Three offensive men play set positions (Diagram 10). Passer in corner of center court alternates passing the ball to the three offensive men. Two defensive men try to deflect the pass or intercept. Put a defensive man five feet away from the passer and have him wave his arms and rotate in an arc to bother the passer.

General Comments

The press requires continuing effort and patience because it's a gambling defense. It's possible to fall behind early in the game until you are able to make the minor adjustments to the type of attack being used against the defense. But most teams don't have more than two types of attack versus any press.

The object of the ball press is to force the offense to hurry and thus make errors. However, never reach in and try to take the ball away from the opponent. Play arm's length before the dribble—move in half that distance after the dribble—but don't reach for the ball.

Try to make the offense throw the lob pass or the bounce pass. Don't let them make straight passes out unless they are back towards our own basket. Whenever the ball passes your line of defense—sprint toward the basket until you have passed the ball again—then get back on defense.

Strong side men be alert to double-team. Weak side men be alert for interceptions. Players must be drilled on individual man-to-man fundamentals to make the defense more successful.

If no opponent is in your zone, don't stay there—go to your zone and then adjust to where you can help. Use man-to-man principles if man is in your zone and has the ball—but don't reach in.

You must keep the offense out of the middle in their back court—force it to the side. Attack the ball in your area—in doubt, both men attack. When ball goes inside, attack front and rear.

3

Developing a Strong Man-to-Man Defense

by John Abramczyk

Head Basketball Coach
Eisenhower High School
Blue Island, Illinois

John Abramczyk has been coaching high school basketball for 13 years and has an overall record of 236-80, which includes four conference championships and 15 tournament championships.

Developing an effective man-to-man basketball defense takes a little bit of everything. At our high school we stress the following factors:
pride in the defensive aspect of the game;
fundamentals of play and drills to perfect them;
individual responsibility;
team responsibility.
Here's the way we deal with these aspects.

Building Pride

All coaches instruct their players on stance weight distribution, sliding techniques, covering a man with and without the ball, etc.—but many overlook a very important ingredient that must also be developed—pride.

Each individual player must take pride in his own defense before you can start to build a proper team attitude.

To help in this respect, our coaches make a "big production" in practice situations when a boy makes a particularly good defensive play, or finally perfects a difficult defensive maneuver. Locker room and hallway walls are adorned with defensive slogans. Interviews with the news media, radio, and newspapers are never conducted without covering some aspect of the defense—always including the mention of a name or two.

> **DEFENSIVE STATISTICS: During a game an assistant coach keeps defensive statistics—charting a player each time his defensive maneuver aids or hinders the team. The chart is tabulated, giving us our "top defensive player" of the game. Newspaper reports cite the winner.**

At the conclusion of the season, besides selecting a "Most Valuable Player" and "Captain"—we also present a "Best Defensive Player" award. Naturally, employing such methods is only part of the job. The coach plays a big part also—he must be very enthusiastic in his approach to teaching defense. He must believe in what he does and exhibit a world of confidence in his players.

Teaching Fundamentals

We try to keep the teaching of fundamentals as simple as possible. Our stance is never parallel. We don't have a preference as to which foot is forward—but we do insist on having one foot forward. We tell the boys to drop their weight, with slightly more weight on the back foot than on the front foot. Their knees should be flexed, back relatively straight, hands low and flashing.

> **NOTE: On a fake, any fake, we instruct our boys to go straight off—to drop step. If the ball is dribbled away from the strong foot, we work with our players on the swing step. Drills used to work on these fundamentals follow.**

Wave drill: In our wave drill (Figure 1) the players assume a defensive stance on the court facing a coach who has a ball in his hands. We prefer using a ball and having the players react to its movement rather than reacting to hand signals or verbal commands. Before the movement with the ball is started, the stance of each player is checked.

If the ball is raised above the head, the players are to quickly move forward. If the ball is moved to the right or left side, the players are to slide accordingly. If the coach should quickly move the ball to his hip and step toward the players (simulating an offensive foot take), the boys must retreat quickly.

COACHING POINT: While the drill is being run, the players are constantly being checked for stance, distribution of wieght, not corssing the feet on the slide, etc.

Swing step drill: Our swing step drill is illustrated in Figure 2. The players—in a good defensive stance—begin at one corner and slide step on a diagonal line up the floor. When they get to the line (free-throw lane line or sideline) they quickly swing step and continue their diagonal up the floor in the opposite direction.

Combat drill: This is a quick reaction, fun-type drill. Players pair up in a defensive stance facing one another. At a signal, they are to touch the inside of the knee of their opponent. To be effective, both boys must be moving constantly. They have to stay low, flash those hands out and back—because they have to protect their knees, too, and maintain good body balance.

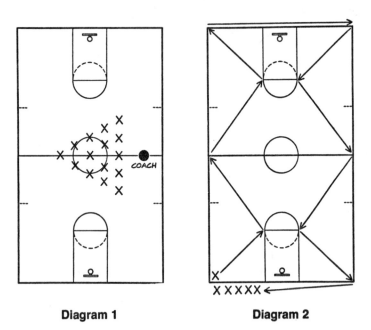

Diagram 1   **Diagram 2**

One-on-one full-court drill: This drill (Figure 3) begins when the defensive man passes the ball to the offensive man who then dribbles the full length of the court—staying within the sideline and the near free-throw lane line. The defensive man plays on the point of the ball, using

Diagram 3

retreating steps, attempting to make the dribbler turn.

For variations, this drill may be used from specific spots on the floor—this time allowing the offensive man to work into position for a shot. The drill may be started from the top of the circle, from the forward position, or on the base line. Also you can have the defensive man grasp a towel that is hanging around his neck, or clasp the hands behind the back until the shot is taken.

Individual Responsibility

Guard on ball: The guard defensing against the offensive player in possession of the ball must attack him. He must not allow the offensive player a choice as to where he wants to go—he must dictate terms to the offensive man.

When he's in this one-on-one situation, his primary responsibility is to force the man to the sideline. He attempts to entice the dribbler all the way to the corner, and when he gets to the base line, he cuts it off, thereby forcing the dribbler to reverse back toward the center of the floor.

> **NOTE: At this point, the defensive men in that area can either come over and trap or, if the man with the ball has picked up his dribble, apply so much pressure on the man they're guarding that it would be very difficult for him to receive a pass.**

Weakside guard: In order to keep our opponents off balance, we try to apply pressure at different positions on different occasions. The weakside guard does his part in trying to frustrate the opposition by either overplaying his defensive assignment, thus preventing his man from receiving a pass, or dropping back off his man.

Strongside forward: This man's responsibility is to overplay his man, preventing a direct pass to him, forcing him to come high or wide toward the sideline to catch the ball. We always want this offensive man moving away from the basket to receive the ball.

Weakside forward: The weakside forward plays off his man in a position where he can see his man and the ball. He supports the post coverage, being particularly alert for the "over-the-top" pass. However, he must not sink so far that he'll go past the middle of the basket, as he'll be in poor position for another area of his responsibility—that of sealing out and fighting for the rebound on that weak side.

Besides assisting in the coverage of the post, this boy must also be ready to give help to teammates, especially if the guards are attempting to set their man up for a trap maneuver. He must also prevent his man from becoming an offensive threat, never allowing him to cut in a straight line—and never permitting him to catch the ball inside the free-throw lane.

Defending the post: If the offensive pivot establishes himself in a low post position, the defender's job is to front him and prevent him from receiving the ball—preferably forcing him out to the 15-foot mark. If the pivot is set as a high post, but without the ball, the defender may loosen up and play on the ball side. If the pivot has the ball in this position, the defender must square up on him and play him tight when he pivots and faces the basket.

Breakdown Drills

We're not satisfied that we've done our job of teaching defense by just working fundamental drills, or telling each player where and how to play, or even scrimmaging. We take some of the basic offensive maneuvers, or some phase of an opponent's offense, and break it down to a drill that can be worked on in practice—so that when that situation occurs during a game, the boy will react automatically and correctly to the maneuver.

> NOTE: Maneuvers, such as splitting the post, guard-around, the weave, pick and roll, cutting off the base line, and stopping the weakside cutter through the lane are all utilized—but from a defensive standpoint.

Whenever instruction is given pertaining to a specific position or a particular technique, or whenever a breakdown drill is run, all players are required to participate. We want each boy to know how to cope with a situation that particularly affects him during a game.

Team Responsibility

While we want our players to develop pride in their individual defense, we also want this pride to carry over to their team defense. We impress upon our boys that the scoreboard reads—"Schlarman High School" not "Davis" or "Jones" or "Miller." Also, our boys know that when the opponent gets a basket—it's scored against all of us, not against a single defender.

4

Pressure Defense Using the 1-3-1

by Robert Basarich

Head Basketball Coach
Central High School
Lockport, Illinois

Robert Basarich has been coaching high school basketball for the past 16 years and has an overall record of 414-99. As head basketball coach at Central, he has an eight-year record of 179-32. This includes five conference titles, five regional titles, and three sectional titles. His teams have participated in three state tournaments (1968, 1972, and 1973).

Our defense is basically a 1-3-1 used from a half-court zone press back into a tight zone. We have variations to meet almost every offensive situation—such as the trap, butterfly, high trap, low trap, semi-tight and many others that are needed throughout a particular game.

NOTE: We have found this defense to be workable against every type of team or offense. In 59 games, only 6 opposing teams have scored 60 or more points against it.

Of course, you need to sell your players on this defense; it doesn't come in a few weeks. They have to be hungry, dedicated, and willing to practice very hard if this defense is to be workable.

Positions: Every position is more important than in a man-to-man defense, because if one man doesn't complete his task the whole defense will collapse.

The point man, P in Diagram 1, should be your smallest player with excellent speed, quickness and desire. He drives the ball in the direction you would like it to go. He also puts constant pressure on the ball. He's the key to your defense, a leader.

Diagram 1

Wing men, 2 and 3 in Diagram 1, are usually your third and fourth tallest men with good hands and speed. These players make more moves than the others—they trap from the ten-second line to the base line; they pitch the 45° angle; they rebound and start the fast break if you have one.

> **TIP: We like our wing men to be from 6'1" to 6'3" and they must like to run and rebound. We also want quickness if possible.**

The center, C in Diagram 1, is the tallest player or the pivot man. In a tight zone, his task is not very difficult compared to the half-court press situation. But this man is always an important key to your defense—he covers the area next to the basket.

> **NOTE: Any mistake here is in the 10-foot to lay-up range. The most important aspects of the center's game are good foot movement, good hands, and strong rebounding.**

The back man, B in Diagram 1, should be 6 feet or taller, should like to run and rebound, and also be a good thinker. He must cover the complete base line from corner to corner. His area is about 50 feet long and 5 feet wide.

> **TIP: The back man must be able to react to the ball and the ball only. If he quits following the offensive setup, there is no way he can physically cover the area for which he's responsible.**

Setup: The point man positions himself in the center jumping circle, while the wing men and center are above the free-throw circle. The back man must be even with or above the dotted line (the lower part of the free-throw circle). From this setup (Diagram 1), your pass trap is a half-court one, at the coffin corners and the baseline corners.

Trapping: This can be done in different ways—for instance, your point man can drive the dribbler in a certain direction. Your wing man can play high to work on guards who are poor ball handlers—or play low against forwards who can't handle the ball well (Diagram 2). Then we would trap the baseline corners.

> **NOTE: Of course, you can always trap with one man and butterfly the other.**

Butterfly: The butterfly situation takes place when you play a team that you can't trap. Diagram 3 shows the positions of each player when the butterfly is in effect.

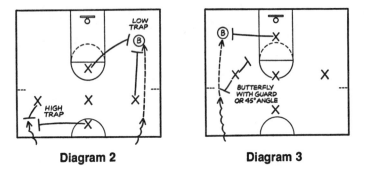

Diagram 2   **Diagram 3**

Tight zone: You use a tight zone for the same reasons that you use any type of zone. But, we feel that because of the position of players in a 1-3-1, it can be a little more effective.

Semi-tight zone: The semi-tight zone is put to use when you play a team that can shoot well from the outside and also pass well. This type of zone pushes the offense beyond the 15- to 20-foot range.

The following points are important to this defense:

1. Four of the five starters must be quick.
2. The point man and back man must have excellent speed.
3. Four of the five starters should be 6'1" or taller.
4. Wing men must be quick and intelligent.
5. Every player must be a worker.

Disadvantages: Naturally, the 1-3-1 has disadvantages such as rebounding difficulty; wing men get caught too high or too low; the baseline or bottom man has a very difficult task; this defense cannot be played soft—it has to be given 100% effort.

Advantages: But there are advantages—it allows you to put pressure on the ball; gives fast break advantages; just good height will suffice; many different types of defenses can be used with it.

5

Picking Up in a Man-to-Man Press from Assigned Zone Areas

by Vince Budenholzer

Head Basketball Coach
Holbrook High School
Holbrook, Arizona

Vince Budenholzer's overall record for 18 years of basket-ball coaching is 272-131. In his last ten years at Holbrook High School, his teams have won nine conference champion-ships. During those ten years, his teams lost only seven con-ference games. His 1971 squad won the state championship and his 1965 squad was the state runnerup. His 1964, 1966, 1967, 1968 and 1973 teams reached the state semifinals.

Most coaches in basketball today employ some form of pressing defense as part of their game plan. Frequently this pressing defense is used only when a change in game tempo is needed to meet a situation which cannot be coped with using the original game plan. For instance, it may be adopted when falling too far behind an opponent, losing momentum, or trying to bring off an upset in the waning minutes of a game.

NOTE: However, we believe that an efficient full-court press can be most effective when used for the entire game, not simply as a resort in situations calling for a turnabout effort.

What does it take? All of us have seen fine coaches with good teams defeated by opponents employing the full-court press throughout the game. How many of these coaches come to the following week's practice or the following season determined to install an equally effective full-court press only to find that they cannot make it work? Often, if the coach is not successful in setting up the effective pressing defense, we hear him say that his material was not suited, or that he would rather build his defense according to the speed, mobility, and ability of his boys than fulfill any desire to run a full-court press.

Though I cannot take issue with such thinking, I do feel that many coaches would be more effective in their use of a pressing defense if they would do some additional planning, make a greater effort to become familiar with this defense, and—above all—use patience in teaching the pressing defense to their ball clubs.

PATIENCE: Patience is stressed, for if you have not emphasized a running and pressing game before, it will require time to teach the skills essential to a consistently effective pressing defense.

Changing to the press: Upon our arrival at Holbrook eight years ago, we immediately began to change the emphasis from a conventional style of defense to the full-court press. We did this at the junior varsity and frosh levels as well as at the varsity level. At the same time we began to stress running, the fast break, and what we call "blitz drills" to make our total pressing game more effective.

RESULTS: In the first three years following this change we did not have a losing season, although we achieved only a break-even record of 34-31. Then our program and stress began to pay off: Our records in the past five years have been 18-8, 17-8, 17-5, 15-8, and 18-3.

Assigning zone areas: A prime ingredient in any successful press is that each player know his assignment in every situation. Thus we devised what I call *man-to-man press picking up from assigned zone areas* (Diagram 1). From each of the assigned areas shown in the diagram, we have one of our players pick up an opposing player, man-to-man. The player picked up varies according to the zone assignment. These assignments take effect immediately after we score or commit a violation under our basket.

The individual zone responsibilities are as follows:

Our strong side (Area 1) is covered by our fastest man because this is the area into which the ball is most often thrown. Usually we cover this area with our strongest, fastest guard.

Our middle area (Area 3) and back zone (Area 4) are normally covered by our tallest guard and post man. The specific assignment depends on each boy's special attributes and abilities.

Our weak side (Area 2) is normally covered by our smallest (and generally fatest) forward.

To prevent the throw-in man (Area 5) from making the long, uncontested pass, we normally use our biggest forward here. His defensive assignment can change from staying with the throw-in man, to double-teaming the offensive man to whom the ball is thrown.

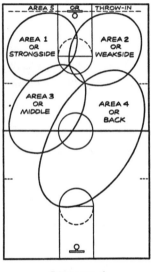

Diagram 1

Objectives: Working from this setup, our initial effort is focused on intercepting the throw-in or causing the offense to throw the ball out-of-bounds. If we are unsuccessful, we apply man-to-man pressure, switching when necessary to force the offense into violations or ball handling mistakes. From this setup, we can remain in a man-to-man defense by staying with the man with whom we cross the half-court line. Or, we may drop into a zone defense, though normally we prefer to stay in a man-to-man defense.

FRONT MEN: The front three players (covering Areas 1, 2, and 5) are usually our best scorers, jump shooters, ball

handlers, etc. They should be effective dribblers and crisp shooters with both left and right hand.

Reacting to situations: Naturally, questions arise, such as what happens when the throw-in team groups the four potential receivers in one area? Or, what happens when the ball is thrown cross-court out-of-bounds, thus creating a new throw-in man? Or, what happens when the throw-in team criss-crosses its men or sets up screening situations? And, quite naturally, in all of these situations we switch assignments as the offense commits itself to movement.

For example, when our defensive player responsible for coverage in Area 1 finds no opposing player in his zone of responsibility, his zone of responsibility then overlaps into the other zones of responsibility. He must find the closest man loose. To help players meet such changing situations effectively, we have established rules which, properly carried out, will mean that the player's closest loose man will usually be quite close to his zone of responsibility if all of his teammates have carried out their own responsibilities according to our rules. (The rules vary somewhat from year to year depending on available personnel.)

PRACTICE: Practice against all of the known and common attacks used to combat the press is important. It is also important to discuss, teach, and practice carrying out each player's assignment in harmony with the different situations his team may encounter.

Setting game tempo: In running this type of press, we know that we are going to make mistakes. But we feel that we can make our opponents commit more mistakes than we do since this is our game. We are confident that we will be in a better position to capitalize on our opponents' mistakes than they will be to capitalize on ours. With our pressing and running game, we feel confident that our opponents are less able to effectively use unconventional defenses, offenses, traps, etc., against us and that we will be in a better position than they to dictate the pace of the game.

6

The 1-3-1 Matching Zone and Man-to-Man

by William T. Boylan

Head Basketball Coach
Monmouth College
West Long Branch, New Jersey

In 17 years as head basketball coach (and athletic director) at Monmouth College, William Boylan has never had a losing season, amassing 295 wins against 125 losses. In the last four seasons (101-16) his clubs have won three district NAIA championships and garnered him two "Coach-of-the-Year" awards. In a nine-year span, Monmouth has won seven Central Atlantic College Conference championships. Coach Boylan is president of the Metropolitan College Basketball Coaches' Association.

No defense will hold a team scoreless. Rather than courting the frustration of striving for the impossible, we have established the resasonable goal of holding the opposition to the low sixties. We want to cut their percentage of good shots. Since we play almost all "pattern" teams, our defense is aimed at not allowing a team to play its pattern.

TIP: The man playing the ball handler may apply extreme pressure without attempting to steal the ball. Make him react to you; don't let him pass when he wants, where he

wants, or to whom he wants. Pressure will cause mistakes such as walking or poor passing.

The Next Logical Receiver

The man playing the next logical receiver should play between his man and the ball just enough to prevent a pass. If the opponent goes for the basket, go with him while facing the ball, keeping between the ball and the man while traveling toward the basket and help.

Players covering men other than the next logical receiver should slough off as far as possible toward the middle, clogging up play and giving help when needed. At all times they should be able to see the man they are playing and the ball, with the chance of getting a hand on the ball if it's passed to their man.

NOTE: In teaching our defense, we first look at it as a complete team defense, then break it into its individual parts, and finally put it together as an operating whole.

Individual Duties

The area covered by our point man, X1, is shown in Diagram 1. Our most agile shorter man, he tries to make the offense go to one side or the other, to overload and play on one quarter of the court. This cuts in half the area to defend and when ten men are matched up in a quarter of the court, it's too clogged for an offense to move freely or keep passing lanes open.

The point man must resist traveling more than a step or two from the top of the key, as some offenses will rotate a man into the top from the weakside wing. Areas A and B in the diagram indicate danger zones for

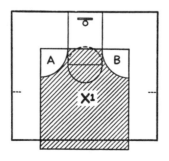

Diagram 1

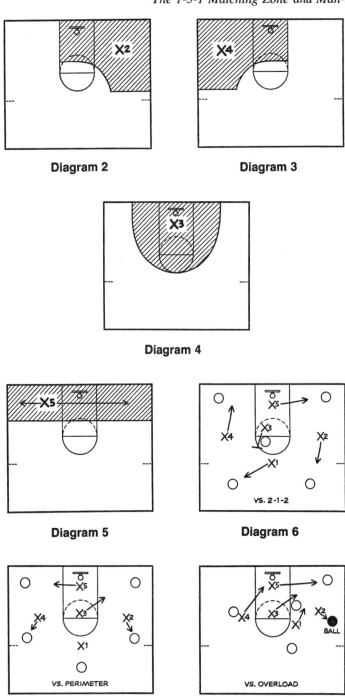

Diagram 2   Diagram 3

Diagram 4

Diagram 5   Diagram 6

Diagram 7   Diagram 8

the point man to enter. X1 should also be ready to double-team if the guard bringing the ball down passes to a wing but doesn't move for a give-and-go.

Diagram 2 details the area covered by wing man X2, who is tall and a good rebounder. He picks up the opposing wing man, guards him closely when he is the next logical receiver and pressures him when he has the ball. If his man cuts, he stays with him to the next area until the next man is ready to pick him up.

The other wing man, X4, has the same duties on the opposite side of the court, the area shown in Diagram 3.

Our center, X3, generally plays the man in the high or low post (Diagram 4), attempting to deny him an incoming pass. He overplays his man by at least a half, but moves 100% in front of him in the pivot or under the basket. He may loosen up on a very weak player or when the opponent goes to the top of the key.

Finally, our X5 or back man—the second shortest player—plays both corners (Diagram 5). As the area covers both sides of the court he must be alert for the ball being reversed. Normally he plays the corner man on the strong side. In case of a perimeter attack, when opponents set up in both corners, X5 picks the shorter man and X3 defends the other corner.

Pressure Most Important

Pressure on the ball is crucial, especially when a team attempts to rotate the ball from one corner to the other. With X5 covering both corners, the ball must be slowed down.

Diagrams 6, 7 and 8 demonstrate moves against 2-1-2, perimeter and overload attacks.

TIP: The defensive quarterback can make this defense exceptionally tough if he judiciously makes use of the device of calling "freeze" or "hold" or other key word: all defenders then play man-to-man with the offensive man they are matched up with at the moment.

With practice, these defensive rules will apply admirably to a half-court pressing man-to-man defense—simply forget the area limits that apply to the zone.

7

The 1-2-2 Zone Defense: Ideas and Techniques

by Carl M. Grimsrud

Head Basketball Coach
Elkton High School
Elkton, Oregon

During his 27 years at Elkton High Coach Grimsrud has seen his share of victories. His squads have won four state championships and hold the state record for consecutive basketball victories–51, set in 1963, 1964, and 1965. His overall record is 456-160.

Although we have always believed in the man-to-man as our basic defense, our teams have used the zone defense with considerable frequency the last several seasons.

NOTE: We first used a 2-1-2 zone and were not very happy with the results. There seemed to be two main problems:

1. Opposing teams always seemed to come up with at least one "sharpshooter" who would shatter our defense by scoring heavily from the open areas on the sides, out from the free-throw line.

2. Our player material always seemed to be such that we would have at least one short player in the lineup, too short to play the front line of the 2-1-2 zone effectively.

1-2-2 ZONE: As a result of such experience, we decided to try the 1-2-2 zone and were pleasantly surprised at how much more effective it proved to be than our version of the 2-1-2. We found that:

1. The shorter player who had difficulty doing an effective job on the front line of the 2-1-2 zone could play the point on the 1-2-2 zone quite effectively—and also could harass the offensive team as they tried to set up their offense much more than we had been able to do from the 2-1-2 zone.

2. We seemed to be able to cover the side spots out from the free-throw line much better.

3. We had been concerned that we would not be able to cover the open spots at the free-throw line. This has not proved to be the case; however, this may be due to the fact that we have not seen very many teams with good and big high-post players.

Initial lineup: When we first used the 1-2-2 zone we did not have any players over 6'1" tall. Our four players in the 2-2 ranged from 5'11" to 6'1"—however, they are all fairly quick and could jump quite well.

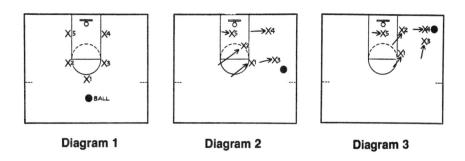

| Diagram 1 | Diagram 2 | Diagram 3 |

NOTE: See Diagram 1 for the initial lineup when the offensive team has the ball out in front. The point player was 5'6" and was very quick.

Initial shift: With this group the shift we used was as indicated in Diagrams 2 and 3. As the ball is moved to the right side, X2 moves diagonally toward the end line keeping in line with the ball; that is, on the line from the ball to the basket. X3 covers the ball; X1 starts to drop toward the high-post area; X4 starts toward the corner; X5 steps up toward the front of the basket.

As the ball gets to the corner, X2 has continued his move and is in the

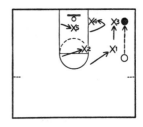

Diagram 4   **Diagram 5**

low-post area and also must be prepared to guard the end line; X4 is covering the ball in the corner; X5 is at the front of the basket; X1 is in the high-post area, X3 is guarding the side and/or double-teaming the ball. When the ball goes to the left corner, X5 covers to the corner and X3 shifts back diagonally to the low post and end-line area on that side.

> **NOTE: If a post man receives the ball from out front, in the middle post area, either X2 or X3 covers between the ball and the basket. X1 collapses on the ball. If the ball comes in from any point left of the top of the key, X3 covers the ball. If the ball comes in from any point right of the key, X2 has the responsibility to cover between the post man with the ball and the basket (Diagram 4).**

Shift adjustments: When our type of players changed and we had two bigger but not as quick players to fit into our 1-2-2 zone, we found our shift resulted in taking our taller boys too far away from good rebounding position—and because of their lack of quickness, they were usually unable to get back into position in time to do much good on the boards.

At the X5 and X4 positions we stationed 6'4" and 6'5" players. Now X3 shifts with the ball all the way to the corner as the ball comes in on offense on the right side (Diagram 5). X2 covers the high-post area on the right of the key. X1 covers the right side. X4 covers the low post and guards the endline and X5 takes the front of the basket and guards the weak side of the basket.

> **NOTE: If the ball goes into the left corner, X2 shifts to the corner with the ball.**

Player responsibility: This type of shift, in order to be effective, demands that both X2 and X3 be very quick players. We placed our quickest and best defensive player at the X3 position because most of our opponents seemed to prefer to run their offenses to their right side. The fact that X3 was left-handed also seemed to be a defensive help—as he was

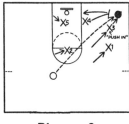 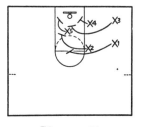

Diagram 6   **Diagram 7**

more effective covering on the side and in the corner against jump-shooters, especially when he was forced to cover hurriedly.

> **NOTE: The fact that X2 was right-handed seemed to help also in covering to the left corner for similar reasons.**

On situations where long, over-the-top passes or quick reverses get the ball to the corners (or sides) very quickly, X4 or X5 (depending on which side the ball comes) must cover the ball. Even then, however, we call for X3 or X2 to "push" their way in and for X4 or X5 to fall back to the low-post area. If X3 or X2 is very late in coming, he is to cover in the low-post area (Diagram 6).

> **NOTE: One very significant point is that regardless of who covers the corner, he is a very important rebounder and must make every effort to get back to the boards. We particularly stress that the player in the corner, when the ball goes up to the boards, should "hook" to the front of the boards and not try to crash straight in on the side (Diagram 7).**

Summary: We believe that the 1-2-2 zone gives us good defensive balance. All four players in the 2-2 have primary defensive rebounding responsibilities—and in this zone they can easily react to their areas of responsibility.

We liked the 1-2-2 zone particularly well because the point man can gamble to a considerable degree and the rest of the defense is still sound. He can harass and chase the ball while the offensive team is bringing it up the floor.

It is one zone defense where the small player, if he is quick and well-conditioned, can be a great asset and not a weak-spot in the defense as he might be in some of the other zone defenses. The 1-2-2 is especially effective when you have a dedicated, tireless type of ballplayer in the point position.

8

A Zone and Man-to-Man Combination Defense to Stop the Good Outside Attack

by Loring Vance, Jr.

Head Basketball Coach
Paw Paw High School
Paw Paw, West Virginia

Loring Vance, Jr. has been coaching basketball for 13 years–12 years at Mathias High School (Mathias, West Virginia) and 1 year at Paw Paw High School. He has an overall record of 269 wins against 196 losses. In 1969, Vance was named Potomac Valley Conference "Coach-of-the-Year." At present, he is again the head basketball coach at Mathias High School.

After being soundly throttled by our arch-rival, we sought to devise a defense that would offset three excellent outside shooters and a mediocre inside attack.

By putting our three best defenders on the three outside shooters, and taking them man-for-man after they crossed the mid-court line, we were able to cut down their point production by 25 points and defeat them handily. This defense can easily be sold to diligent players. It will also provide the chance to over-play the good outside shooters and clog up the middle if they drive to the basket.

NOTE: Most of the teams that we play set only the single pick and we switch when we recognize this coming up—the back defender calling the switch whenever possible. I believe that it would be possible for aggressive defenders to break up a double or triple pick.

The two bigger men are lined up side by side with arms extended as far as possible, taking up as much room as possible. They guard the other team's bigger (and less mobile) men when they come close to the basket on a zone basis.

Basic setup: Figure 1 shows the basic setup of 3 (man-to-man) and 2 (zone) defense. X4 and X5 stay in tandem zone while X1, X2 and X3 play tight man-to-man defense.

NOTE: It is the responsibility of the two playing zone to pick up any driver who gets through the outside defenders and cut off his path to the basket.

Single pick: If a single pick is used on X2 (Figure 2), X5 must move out to the top of the key, stop the drive and force the shot outside while X4 fills his vacant area. X1 sloughs off to further clog the middle area. X3 slides through and picks up his own man as soon as possible.

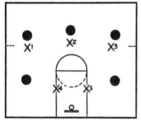

Diagram 1

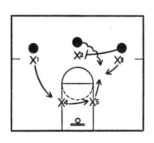

Diagram 2

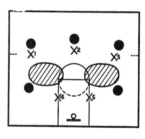

Diagram 3

NOTE: As stated, the weakside defender (X1) can slough off and clog up the middle. It also helps if he is a good rebounder. You may crash all five men for the missed shot or depend upon X4 and X5 for the bulk of the board work and send X1, X2 and X3 down on the fast break.

Set up your best two rebounders under the basket and your three quickest defenders on the three outside men. Our opposition had not seen this defense when we first used it and they were completely baffled.

Weakest area: The area around the foul-line extended (Figure 3) seems to be the weakest link in this defense. But hustle and arms high will compensate somewhat for this. Sloughing off by the weakside guard helps too. In the corners we overplay the good shooter and have the zone men pick him up.

If their inside men go to the corners to shoot, X4 will follow to his corner while X5 will move to the 3-second area. Same rule applies to the other side. Remember, the most difficult spots to shoot from are the corners.

> **NOTE: This defense has been very successful for us in tournament games and our boys have responded by winning five of the seven games in which we have chosen to show the opposition this particular type of defense. I would recommend saving it for the second game against a particular team.**

If one of the outside men moves to the corner and your scouting reports indicate that this corner shooter is particularly effective if given time to shoot—your defensive man-to-man player can overplay his man to the right or left. This overplay can also be used in your basic setup of this defense because your two zone men are always there to pick up the driver if he gets by his man-to-man defender.

9

A Repertoire of Zone Presses

by Walt Milroy

Head Basketball Coach
Ingraham High School
Seattle, Washington

In a school just thirteen years old, Walt Milroy has compiled an overall 175-96 won-lost record. His 1969 squad was the greatest: an undefeated season (23-0) and the State AAA championship. Coach Milroy's squads have won or tied for the championship four times in the last six years.

Although familiar with many types of defense, we rely mainly on variations of the zone press. This means being ready to play basketball all over the court—not just at one end. We practice this defense every day and against every conceivable attack. No other school prepares against pressure as well as we prepare to apply it.

POTENT WEAPON: Games are turned quickly. With the zone press at your disposal, you are never out of any contest. But your players must get the entire picture of what you are doing as a team; otherwise, the defense will not work.

This type of defense play features several definite advantages:
- It allows us to control the pace of the game. We want a fast pace, and

this forces a fast pace. While other schools prefer a definite pattern game, we are accustomed to playing a running game.

• Our defense forces the opposition to play something they are not used to playing.

• Their players are forced to shoot from positions and spots they do not usually shoot from. This is very distracting.

Further, the zone press defense allows us to go quickly from defense to offense. Many passes are intercepted, creating easy fast-break opportunities.

The 2-2-1 Zone Press

Our special baby is the 2-2-1 press. It is the most identifiable part of our game and the part most responsible for our success (other than material). We run it all the time—in back-court, front-court, warm-up drill, and in the locker room! Our opponents would agree it's not much fun to play against.

The full-court 2-2-1 is demonstrated in Diagram 1. We allow the pass

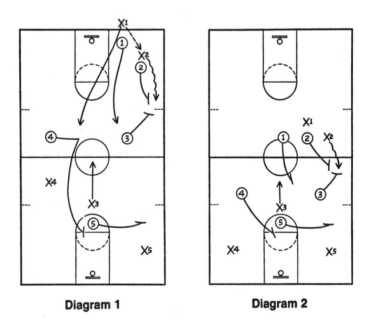

Diagram 1   Diagram 2

in to X2, but 1 prevents a return pass to X1 while 2 allows X2 to dribble down the sideline (preferably the left). 3 moves up to challenge and stop X2's dribble, and 2 then traps X2.

1 falls back to mid-court to prevent or intercept passes to X1 or X3. 5 moves over to the sideline to prevent or intercept a pass to X5. 4 fakes to mid-court and quickly moves into the safety area. He is the one who has many opportunities for interception.

> **MOTIVE: The trapper and challenger are not looking so much to steal the ball or tie up the dribbler; they want to force an "interceptable" lob pass. It is better to intercept than to prevent. So 1, 4, and 5 should "show" an opportunity to the trapped man, then move in to intercept as soon as he commits himself. This does not mean after the ball is in the air—you can usually tell when and where a player is going to pass.**

Minor adjustments may be made to handle different ways teams attack the zone press.

The Half-Court 2-2-1

In the half-court 2-2-1 (Diagram 2), we "invite" X2 across mid-court—preferably on his weak side. 3 then challenges and 2 traps. Don't let X2 dribble between 2 and 3 or outside of 3.

1 prevents a pass to X1 and especially to X3, the key player in most team attacks. 5 goes to the sideline to intercept or prevent a pass to X5. 4 becomes the safety and must intercept or prevent any pass to X4.

This defense is very effective. Once X2 is across mid-court and trapped, he cannot pass back without a violation. He often panics and a turnover results. The pass to X3 must not be completed. 4 and 5 have many interception possibilities. As soon as an interception occurs, everyone *goes*, with an offensive job to do.

> **DANGER: Fouling is a serious defensive error. It destroys our whole concept because it causes inaction instead of action. Fouling is a direct result of poor position. Examples: flailing at the ball handler, crowding from behind, reaching in improperly. Players often establish proper position but then lose it, and in their effort to re-establish position, they cause contact.**

Another danger is being too conservative. We want to force action. Caution will not create action. We are always on "offensive"—we must have the ball. In order to get it we must be daring. We score more because of errors that our pressure causes the offense to commit.

The 1-1-2-1 Zone Press

The second zone press, the 1-1-2-1, is shown in Diagram 3. Again X1 is allowed to pass in to X2 and X2 is encouraged to dribble down the sideline on his weakest side. 3 challenges and 2 traps, being careful not to foul, by keeping good position and not reaching in. 1 prevents a pass to X3, 5 tries to intercept a pass to X5. 4 falls back to the basket, looking to intercept a pass to X4.

In a variation, 4 prevents a pass to X3 and yells to 1 to "get back under!" This gives the defense more movement.

> **TIP: This defense is used when the offense is having success in completing passes to X3. When the ball gets to the offensive forecourt, we automatically shift to our half-court 2-2-1.**

The 3-1-1 Press

The last of our zone press trio, 3-1-1, is depicted in full-court form in Diagram 4. This defense puts as much backcourt pressure as possible on the offense, and should force long passes.

1 harasses X1 as much as possible, making him work to get the ball in. If the pass is completed, he helps trap the dribbler.

3 and 2 overplay X3 and X2, making them work to receive a pass.

Diagram 3

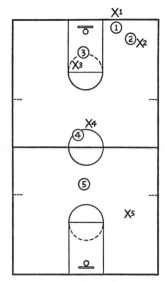

Diagram 4

Again, if a pass is completed, they help trap with 1. If X2 gets the ball, 3 moves to the area into which X2 will probably pass. 4 is alert to intercept any lob pass and 5 is watching for a long pass.

Diagram 5 is the 3-1-1 Lineman Trap. This is worked on either side of the floor, but the basic rule is for 1 always to be the trapper. 2 (or 3, whoever is away from the inbounds pass) overplays the offense near the head of the key. 4 and 5 generally will move in the directions indicated; their movements will be determined by the movements of the offensive deep men. All players should overplay and anticipate. *Invite a pass, then swoop in and intercept it.*

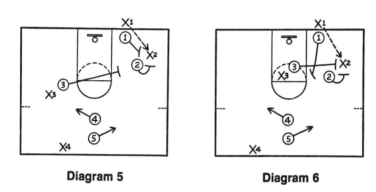

Diagram 5   Diagram 6

THE CHASER TRAP is shown in Diagram 6, again worked on either side of the floor. The difference from the lineman trap is that the chaser away from the inbounds pass becomes the trapper, while the onside chaser is the challenger. The lineman falls back after the inbounds pass and overplays possible receivers. 4 and 5 follow the same rules as for the lineman trap—that is, overplay the offensive men in the area and look to intercept.

Special Defensive Situations

Three special defensive situations are covered by Diagram 7. When up against a two-on-one (7A), the defender fakes at O1 to make him commit himself, then gets back quickly to prevent or intercept to pass to O2. Make O1 shoot from the outside; don't allow O2 to have an easy lay-up. Don't try to check O1 or he'll pass to O2 for the lay-up.

In Diagram 7B the defender is faced with a three-on-one. He fakes at O1 to stop his dribble, then fakes back at O2 to force O1 to pass to O3. Move decisively to prevent or intercept the pass to O3. Don't let the

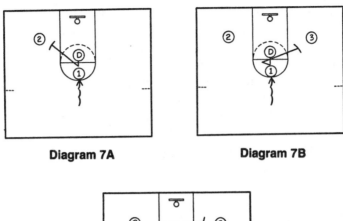

Diagram 7A   **Diagram 7B**

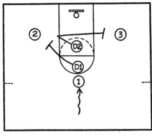

Diagram 7C

offense fake and control you; try to make them commit. Don't leave your feet unless *sure* the shot is going up.

In a three-on-two situation (Diagram 7C), defender 1 challenges the dribbler to stop him, while D2 fakes covering O2 and moves to cover O3. D1 moves back to cover O2. Again, don't leave your feet prematurely; play tough until you can get help. Two good men can often stop three or four.

> **GENERAL RULE: In all these situations where the defense is outnumbered, the safety man will challenge the ball while the help coming back goes to the basket area.**

10

Match Ups and Simple Moves from the 1-2-2

by Frank Milner

Head Basketball Coach
East Orange High School
East Orange, New Jersey

Frank Milner has been coaching high school basketball since 1939, and has compiled an overall record of 384 wins against 187 losses. Head basketball coach at East Orange High School (East Orange, New Jersey), his teams have won six league and conference championships in two different leagues, three sectional state championships, and three state championships in two different groupings. Coach Milner is active in numerous sports associations.

For many years I was convinced that man-to-man defense was the only answer to building a team defense. After a long period of years playing both man-to-man and straight zone defenses, I eventually changed with the times to what is now referred to as a match up defense. I am convinced more than ever that the latter type of defense has so much more to offer in confusing offenses.

NOTE: The term "match up defense" has come into vogue in recent years and has as many different connotations as there are coaches employing it. It actually commences as a

stereotyped zone defense and then changes into a man-to-man coverage on a set signal while still maintaining zone principles. Its strength lies in the fact that every offensive position is closely guarded, yet defensive assignments are continually changing as the offense changes its structure.

Instituting the Defense

In order to institute this type of defense, basic zone teachings must follow man-to-man defense drills. Neither defense must be slighted if good results are to be obtained. Your players must be convinced that match ups are not as difficult as they may seem at first glance.

What destroys the effectiveness of the matching process is the continuous cutting of some offenses that allows men to take short jump shots as the defense scrambles to match up. We feel that when our match up is being attacked by a cutting offense, it's best to switch back to a standard type of zone.

> **EXAMPLE: For example, if we are in a straight zone such as a 1-2-2 and a team proceeds to utilize an overload type of offense, we match up. However, with a cutting type of offense, we sometimes prefer to stay in a standard zone as match ups may prove difficult until such time as match ups may be made with further study during time-outs.**

Basic 1-2-2 Alignment

Diagram 1: This shows the basic 1-2-2 alignment and positions of the players on the floor.

Our two best rebounders will be placed in the 4 and 5 positions as they will do the bulk of the rebounding. The third best board man we like to place in the 2 spot as most teams will go to their right which means that 2 will generally be either sliding in a straight zone on the weak side or matching up in the keyhole area. This will then put us in good rebounding position in most situations.

The 3 man is generally one of our two guards and adept at tight one-on-one defense and also exceptional at interceptions and steals. Our 1 man is our chaser who is also our best stealer, quickest man (since he has generally the biggest slide in a straight zone alignment), and generally our fastest man. He should be a man who can overplay on defense and have the speed to make up lost ground on occasion.

NOTE: We spend a great deal of time with our hands up in the air. We stress the fact that the hand nearest the sidelines should be well up and your opposite hand should extend into the lane. It is important that all personnel concentrate on discouraging the interior pass generally and specifically the pass into any pivot position that the offense will want to set up. We spend a great deal of time drilling on this aspect.

Diagram 2: In most offenses that are employed against a zone, an overload is used with a strong-size pivot. When this occurs, and the penetrating pass is made on the offensive right, the weak-side board man (4) must move to cut off the pivot area and cover as shown in Diagram 2. If the ball is moved to the left side of the offense, the other baseline defender (5) will make the identical move on the opposite side of the floor.

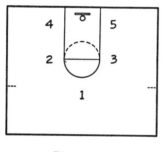 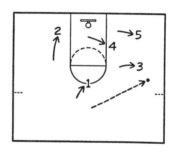

Diagram 1   **Diagram 2**

In Diagram 2, defensive player 2 will immediately attack the ball in a man-to-man position. Player 3 also knows that there will always be the possibility of a pass back to the "handle" of the offense and he should continually be looking for a possible interception on it.

Player 1 who is playing a straight-away defense on a one-man outside handle will jam the middle, also always looking for the easy interception and helping out on fronting the pivot man to a degree—particularly if a team concentrates on getting the ball to an outstanding pivot man. Our 5 man will normally move to cover a possible corner offensive man who might be stationary or possibly cutting into this corner.

NOTE: In Diagram 2, if no offensive player is present, 4 will float into this area to cut off the passing lane to a possible cutter. If a pivot man is present, which is the usual

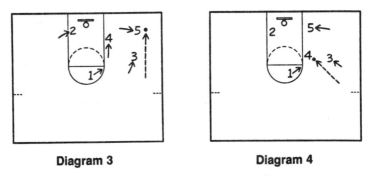

Diagram 3   **Diagram 4**

situation, he will play the offensive side of the pivot man in
an overplay position. He should get his body into such a
position as to have his left hand and left foot nearest the
ball in an effort to get the pivot man to move away from
this area. Player 2 should move to a low baseline position,
matching up with any weakside offensive player as well as
sliding toward the lane. He is also our weakside rebounder
and must try to get inside position for any shot which is
made by the offense.

Diagram 3: This shows what happens when the ball gets into the corner
with 5 playing the ball in a man-to-man move. Player 3 has to come down
inside to discourage the corner offensive man from getting the ball into
the pivot man. Players 1 and 2 slough into the lane and match up with
weakside offensive players.

Diagram 4: In Diagram 4 we show what happens if the ball gets inside
to the pivot man. Player 4 will change to a position directly behind the
pivot while 1 and 2 slough toward the pivot man attempting to make his
movements limited so that he has to pass the ball back out to the safety
handle or try to make his pass to a lower area of the forecourt where our
other defenders should be alert for a possible rushed pass and consequently an interception.

Reversal of Defensive Movements

Diagram 5: One of the most difficult moves to make is that of the
baseline defenders when a switch of the ball from right to left of the court
makes it necessary for a switch of defenders on the pivot man. This is
particularly true if the ball is passed deep into the opposite corner of the
court and 4 must leave the pivot man to pick up the corner offensive
threat.

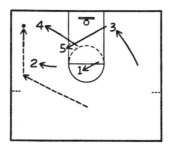

Diagram 5

NOTE: Player 5 must be alert to come up high and switch over to the pivot defense as 4 leaves and goes deep into the corner. This move must be made with a minimum of danger defensively as 3 must slide down to protect the board on the new weakside. Diagram 5 shows this reversal of defensive movements.

This scissoring action between 4 and 5 must be continuously practiced to be highly successful. Match ups such as these are extremely effective against stationary offenses that depend upon movement of the ball rather than movement of personnel.

However, we have found that even against offenses that will send a man through the defense on a cut to an overload position, it still works fairly well. We will let our wing-man defender follow the cutter at least halfway down into the defense to keep him honest so that no pass is made to him in this area. When he declares himself by cutting into an overload spot, then the weakside defender will talk to his teammates in the overload area to alert them to the new alignment.

NOTE: Most of the time a quick switch of personnel can be made to adjust the match up without too much confusion.

Match Up Alignment

In our match up zone defense, we have a man in every area where there's an offensive man. To a certain extent, it's identical to a sinking or sagging man-to-man. If the offensive team is in a 1-3-1, our defense is in a 1-3-1; if the offense is in a 2-1-2, our defense will be the same.

KEYS: The keys we use are usually called by one of our baseline defenders who will use such verbal calls as "21" for 2-1-2 offense; "12" for 1-2-2; "13" for a 1-3-1 and "23" for a 2-3 offense. Diagram 6 shows our match up alignment when an offense sets up with a 2-out guard offense.

Player 1, our chaser, will drop back to line himeself up with 3 in a match up with their two guards. Players 2 and 5 will be responsible for the offensive wing men with 4 picking up their pivot man.

Diagram 7: Here we see what happens if one of the offensive guards cuts into an overload position in a corner out. Player 3 will follow the cutter halfway and call the switch, with 5 taking over the cutter and 3 switching to the wing man who has the ball from the outside guard. Player 1 will still have outside responsibility on the safety man while 2 and 4 will keep their match ups from getting a pass into the vulnerable area.

Diagram 8: This shows the adjustment the inside man makes if the guard changes corners after he has gone through. The baseline defender who took him in the first corner will have to talk to the middle man, 4, to tell him that the offensive man is coming across the back of the zone. You can either have the middle man, 4, make the switch, or decide that the weakside baseline man, 2, pick him up with the others making the match up switches accordingly.

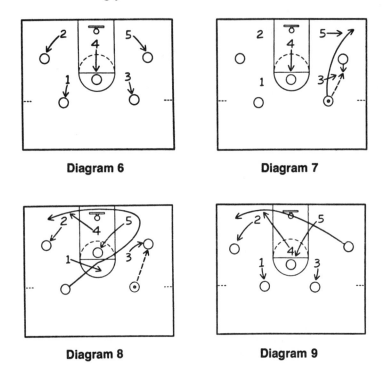

Diagram 6   Diagram 7

Diagram 8   Diagram 9

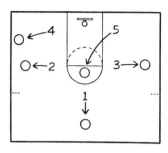

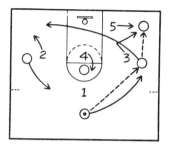

Diagram 10   **Diagram 11**

NOTE: It is a good idea not to change the defenses when a cutter is in the process of going through—but only after movement of the offense has temporarily ceased.

Diagram 9: Here we see the coverage of the offensive wing when he cuts across the defense to the other side of our zone. Player 4 will make the scissor switch on the overload cutter with 5 coming high to take the pivot defense; player 3 sags back with 2 playing man-to-man with the strongside wing.

Diagram 10: In Diagram 10 we show the match up assignments if the offense presents a 1-3-1. The weakside baseline defender must defense the pivot man immediately. He should be aware of this the minute he finds himself "guarding air" as we call it.

Diagram 11: In the event of a rotation of this 1-3-1 as is often the case, we will attempt to double-team the pass to the baseline. As the offensive wing man makes his pass to the deep man, he cuts through and 3 will form a double-team on the ball after he takes a few steps in with the cutter to keep him honest. The weakside defender wing will drop back to check the cutter as he cuts through (Diagram 11).

Summary

The secret to this type of defense is quickness and hustle. Players must continually be alert to defensive switches; they must continually talk to each other. The chief responsibility for talking is generally placed on the inside men who have the job of informing the outer defense of their defensive switches.

11

A Good Pressing Defense from All Areas of the Floor

by Charles Field

Assistant Basketball Coach
Towson State College
Baltimore, Maryland

Charles Field, Jr. has been coaching in the high school and college ranks since 1959. He has coached football, basketball, and baseball at the following schools: St. Leo Prep Military School (Belmont, North Carolina); St. Mary's High School (Annapolis, Maryland); Annapolis High School (Annapolis, Maryland); Anne Arundel Junior College (Severna Park, Maryland). Coach Field has been an assistant coach in basketball and baseball for the past seven years at Towson State College (Baltimore, Maryland). At present, he is the head baseball coach and assistant professor of physical education at Towson State.

It's my feeling that if you have a good zone press and/or man-to-man press, your team will always be in the game and often will rally. The greater the team speed, the larger the area of the court over which the defense may be exerted.

NOTE: The key to the successful man-to-man press is the guards. The full-court press will be effective with great speed and agility at this position. With something short of

these qualities, the half-court man-to-man or the zone press can be brought into play with equal effectiveness.

The zone press requires a smaller degree of specialization than the man-to-man press and it's possible to operate an effective zone press with less defensive ability. The zone press affords the coach the opportunity to "hide" some slow moving personnel (not too many, however) and still get an effective job done. Of course, the zone press will operate most effectively with top notch personnel.

Basic Alignment

Again, it's my feeling that if you use the basic alignment of the 3-1-1 zone press and teach one set of rules and movements you can vary it enough for four or five different presses. You could use the bigger men up front on the full-court zone and the smaller men on the 3-1-1 half-court press.

This full-court press could simply be moved back towards midcourt in order to stop the passes going to the corners near midcourt. In other words, the flexibility of the 3-1-1 press has allowed you to shorten the press passes.

> **TEACHING TIPS: The press is not by any means easy to teach and you could become disappointed easily. However, the coach must have patience, know it thoroughly, and work hard at it. Eventually, the players will get the idea, like it and run it well. There are many holes in any zone press and it can always be beaten on paper, but actually doing it is something else. Give your opponents something to worry about throughout the season after you have prepared it well.**

Overall Objective

1. There should be an all-out effort by each man on the court.

2. Each player should expend all energy to achieve victory.

3. The personal development of each player should be considered.

4. All-out hustle is necessary for a pressing type defense.

5. Coaches must teach defense every day regardless of the previous experience of the player.

6. The coach must be convinced that the type of defense used is the best for his situation and this must be sold to the players—who must believe that they can win with the defense.

7. Defense can make up for sub-par material.

8. Defense slogans and posters should be used to develop the proper attitude.

Pressing Defense Advantages

1. It hinders shooting and constantly keeps the offense off balance.

2. The press is especially effective against screening, pattern, and zone teams.

3. It makes a boy a much better baseball player by developing his abilities to potential.

4. It makes for a more versatile player than the one who has backed up and played zone or man-to-man.

5. The press forces the best players into mistakes.

6. Coaches of opponents playing a pressing team spend three-quarters of their practice sessions trying to combat it. It disrupts their practices entirely.

7. Your players really love to play a pressing game—they take great pride in their ability to press.

8. It makes for great teamwork and conditioning.

9. If your offense is having a bad night, your defense will carry you.

10. The press is offense within itself. It takes pressure off your offense.

11. It gives a sub-par shooter a chance to play because of his defensive ability.

12. It teaches a player to make a quick change from offense to defense.

13. A pressing defense makes a boy more alert because it gives him more freedom and reduces tension.

14. You can use more boys in the lineup—which is always good for morale.

Pressing Defense Disadvantages

1. A pressing defense will commit more fouls than usual.

2. When pressing all over the floor you leave more room for the opponent's maneuver.

3. If one man fails to carry out his assignment, you have defeated your purpose.

4. A pressing team must have adequate reserve power.

5. A player becomes exhausted quicker pressing than he does with any other defense.

6. A team must have average or better speed and agility to press effectively.

7. Some coaches just don't have the personnel to press.

8. A good ball-handling team is hard to press—also, true if a team has an outstanding dribbler.

Situations Calling for the Press

1. When trailing in the latter part of the game.

2. Against a poorly conditioned team.

3. Against a weak ball-handling team.

4. Against a team that uses a slow and deliberate attack and you want to speed up the tempo.

5. Especially effective against inexperienced teams.

6. As a surprise element.

7. When you are blessed with 10 or 12 average or better players.

8. When you have a small team and you're trying to offset the other team's height.

9. After free throws and at the close of a quarter.

10. When players are tight or to give the opponent something to think about.

11. Before half-time to give the opponent something to think about.

12. To counteract an opponent's press.

Points to Emphasize

1. Don't allow the dribbler to penetrate the perimeter of the zone, nor the ball to be passed into the middle.

2. Don't allow the ball to reach the high post at the top of the circle or foul line.

3. Never allow the ball in the low post position for a lay-up.

4. Always have two men on the ball and three others in front of the ball.

Rules to Follow on Each Pass

1. Ball—get the ball but do not foul.
2. Tip—tip the ball back into play if you can't intercept—at least get a hand in there without fouling.
3. Arrive—be there at the same time the opponent and ball arrive, and stop him.
4. Close—close in on him, contain and control him, and force him to the sidelines before help arrives.

ZONE PRESS RESPONSIBILITIES

A. POINT MAN OR #1 POSITION:
1. Guide the direction of a pass or the dribbler to a position favorable to the defense.
2. Double up on the man in possession when the ball is on the front line to your left or right.
3. Protect the middle area of the press when the ball is on the sides or in deep position.
4. Anticipate and deflect or intercept passes at any position on the court as the "drifter."

B. WING MAN OR #2 and #3 POSITIONS:
1. Guide the direction of the dribbler into the front pocket.
2. Prevent the short loop pass over the front line position.
3. Double up on the man with the ball when he's on your side of the court at the side or corner position.
4. Protect under the basket area when the ball is in the opposite corner.
5. Rebound aggressively when under the basket.

C. FLOATER OR #4 POSITION:
1. Prevent pass to high post position to the rear of front line.
2. Double up on man with the ball at side-court position.
3. Protect deep lane position when ball is in corners.
4. Rebound aggressively.

D. BACK MAN OR #5 POSITION:
1. Protect under the basket area against the long or short lay-up pass.
2. Prevent direct pass to low positions.

3. Move out to corner and double up on man with ball in either corner.
4. Rebound aggressively.

Drills to Teach Pressing Defenses

Tag drill: (Diagram 1): Without the ball, the offensive man runs full court trying not to be tagged. If tagged in the chest by the defensive man, he must retreat five yards and start to run and dodge again up court.

NOTE: Stress a good defensive position.

Double-teaming drill (Diagram 2): Two chasers close in on the dribbler forcing him to pick up his dribble. Fundamentals of double-teaming are then stressed.

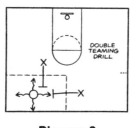

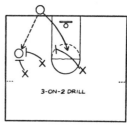

| Diagram 1 | Diagram 2 | Diagram 3 |

EXAMPLE: For example, obstruct but never grab for the ball, knee to knee, hands always moving in direction of the ball.

3-on-2 drill (Diagram 3): As soon as the pass comes in, get a quick double-team; the wing must make sure he fronts the second man and never lets him get it back.

NOTE: Fundamentals of double-teaming are stressed. Don't let the dribbler split the double-team. The drill ends when, and if, the guards get to midcourt.

Sideline double-team drill (Diagram 4): Double-team set at midcourt and the deep corner as the ball is passed down the sideline.
Midcourt double-team drill (Diagram 5): One player in the middle has the ball—is double-teamed quickly and passes to the next line—and the

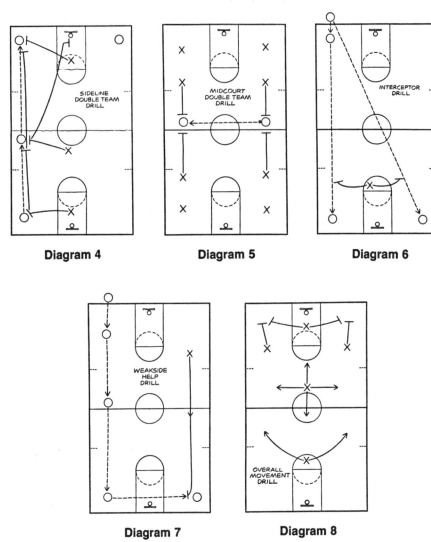

Diagram 4   **Diagram 5**   **Diagram 6**

Diagram 7   **Diagram 8**

double-team is formed as soon as the ball is secured. Never allow the defense to reach in; if they do, blow the whistle and stop the drill.

Interceptor drill (Diagram 6): The back man overplays on the ball side of the court and must react by covering against the full-court pass to either corner.

Weakside help drill (Diagram 7): As soon as the ball passes the front line, the weakside wing man retreats fast to stay in front of the ball. He must ultimately arrive under the basket to prevent an easy lay-up.

Overall movement drill (Diagram 8): Under the rules of zone press responsibilities, players move in unison according to the movements of the ball

12

Two Aggressive Ways to Half-court Trap

by Bob Davis

Head Basketball Coach
Auburn University
Auburn, Alabama

Bob Davis has been coaching college basketball since 1953 and has an overall record of 452 wins against 206 losses, excluding the 30-6 record he holds in International Play. The 1971 "Converse Yearbook" lists him sixth in the nation among the winningest collegiate coaches. Coach Davis began his coaching career at High Point College (High Point, North Carolina), then moved to Georgetown College (Lexington, Kentucky). In 14 years as members of the Kentucky Intercollegiate Athletic Conference, his teams won the season championship nine times, the first place trophy five times, and were runner-up five times. Coach Davis, or Dr. Robert Davis (he received his Ph. D. from Peabody College), has conducted coaching clinics at major colleges throughout the United States, authored numerous articles for major athletic magazines, and recently published a book, "Aggressive Basketball," Parker Publishing Company, West Nyack, New York. In March, 1973, he was appointed head basketball coach at Auburn University.

The most devastating defensive attacks today are the trapping defenses. They are being employed by most championship clubs. The one sure way to control the tempo of a game is to overpower the opponent by pressure and trapping.

> **NOTE: The simple pressure defense without the trap concept is not very effective against the good ball-handling team that has mastered the art of ball control. However, the trap defense will work against all opponents because forced action or ball movement must occur when the trap is clamped on the ball handler. As a matter of fact, the trap will work more effectively against a team that hesitates to initiate movement.**

Definition of the Trap

For the sake of clarification it might be wise to define a trap as it is used in these defenses. A trap occurs when two or more defensive players surround the player who has possession. They generally force the ball handler to move into the portion of the floor where he is placed at greatest disadvantage.

The four corners in front court are the most advantageous places to spring the trap. The defensive team gains two important advantages by trapping in the corners. First, the corner reduces the floor area because the ball handler is partially surrounded by two out-of-bounds lines. Second, this position on the floor allows the team to concentrate the defense and isolate the offensive man furthest from the ball. In Diagram 1 the trap occurs at mid-court, thus isolating O5.

Traps can occur at other spots on the court. However, isolation of an offensive player is harder to achieve and defensive concentration is more dangerous.

> **NOTE: The possible exception is when the trap is sprung in back-court and isolation is achieved by virtue of the length of the court.**

Trap Techniques

Before a team can be successful with the trap defense, there are several techniques that each player must master:

1) Each player must know how to channel his man into a trap area.
2) Each must know how to activate and coordinate a trap action with his teammate. Great hand and foot action is required.
3) Each player who is not involved in the trap action must know

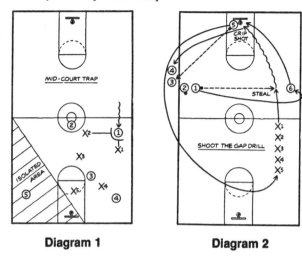

Diagram 1   **Diagram 2**

how to prevent his assigned man and the nearby offensive players from receiving the release pass.

4) Each player must be adept at "reading" the ball handler and anticipating where he will pass.

5) Each player must master the intercept techniuqe.

NOTE: Diagram 2 is a drill used to help players learn how to read the passer and "shoot the gap." O1, O2, and O5 have a ball, and the drill starts by O1 passing to O6 and following the pass to take O6's place. X1 reads O1, intercepts the ball, drives for a crip shot, then takes O4's place. O6 allows X1 to intercept the ball, follows him for the rebound, passes to O4, and goes to the end of the defensive (X's) line.

6) All players must be conscious of recovery and must learn to adjust their floor position while the pass is in the air.

7) When a pass cuts off one or more defensive players, all players must sprint to the basket, or cut-off spot, whichever the case may be. RECOVERY IS THE KEY TO THE SUCCESSFUL TRAPPING DEFENSE.

Full-court Pressing into Half-court Trap

The full-court pressure trap defense can be activated out of the basic man-to-man defensive alignment or any basic zone structure. The various numbered zones, such as 2-2-1 or 1-3-1, are structures that many coaches use.

This writer does not utilize numbers to indicate the zone structure. How the opponent deploys his players will dictate the basic zone structure. All cut-off spots are the same regardless of the zone structure. A cut-off spot refers to the advance point to which all players *sprint* when the ball is moved down the court by the opponent.

> **RULE: It might be wise to insert a rule for these trapping defenses. When one or more defensive players are cut-off by a pass, the trap defense is off until all players have sprinted to primary or secondary cut-off spots, which are well in advance of the ball. This rule holds for the zone or man-to-man defense.**

Man-to-Man Full-court Pressure into Mid-court Trap

This trap is brought about by all defensive players working together to channel the ball handler into a position where a nearby teammate will charge the ball handler for a double-team trap. While the trap is occurring all other teammates are maneuvering into possible cut-off positions.

Pressure is placed on the offensive player who has taken the ball out-of-bounds. This pressure will force the ball handler to look for a close teammate, not having time to throw the long, accurate pass which cuts off defensive players and forces a trap at a secondary spot on the court. The opponent should not be allowed to force the defense to forego any options to trap.

The basic pressure man-to-man defense is employed by all players. The defensive player guarding the man receiving the inbounds pass is instructed to channel his man to the sideline mid-court trap spot. The defensive man on the ball must know where his teammates are and not force the initial trap action until all his teammates are in reasonable intercept positions.

Of course, the defensive players who are preparing to spring the trap must be conscious of maneuvering their men into floor positions which are most hazardous for the offensive team. They must also remember that the defensive player guarding the skilled dribbler has his hands full and cannot help as much as they can.

Assuming the trap is to occur at mid-court, as in Diagram 1, the following floor positions are taken. X1 forces O1 to the sideline and cuts him off as he crosses mid-court. X2 is the closest defensive player; so he charges O1 to activate the trap with X1. X3, X4, and X5 must leave their men and get into "gap shooting" positions. How far they leave their men will depend upon the amount of entrapment achieved by X1 and X2 and the degree of isolation of the other offensive players.

Defensive adjustments are made as the trap is broken by O1. Force is then reapplied and another trap is sprung at a different point, and with different defensive players involved. The defensive team must continuously strive to activate a trap on the player who has possession. This is achieved by channelling and pressing the ball handler into a corner.

Zone Full-court Pressure into Mid-court Trap

As stated earlier, the structure of the zone will depend entirely upon the offensive team. Diagram 3 depicts the 1-3-1 zone pressure attack; however, the mid-court action remains the same regardless of the zone structure employed.

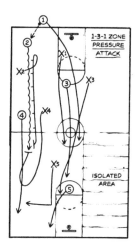

Diagram 3

X1 prevents O1 from throwing the ball inbounds to anyone except O2. X2, X3, X4, and X5 do the same thing in their immediate area of the floor. Once O2 has possession X2 and X1 fake as if they are going to activate an immediate trap. However, X2 is careful to allow O2 to dribble by him while applying half-man cover, which should channel O2 to the trap point at mid-court.

As O2 is dribbling up court, X1, X3, X4, and X5 are maneuvering into trap positions, keeping in mind that all other offensive men must not be allowed to break open for a release pass. When O2 dribbles over mid-court, X4 should be in position to sprint toward O2 and aid X2 in clamping the trap. X5 should be ready to fill for X4. X3 should fill for X5, and X1 should be in position to seal off any cross-court passes.

> **NOTE: It is advisable to practice using several zone structures. The distance to the cut-off spots will vary, but the remaining offensive players will be better covered to prevent release passes.**

Once the offensive team has broken the mid-court trap and has established reasonable order in front-court, the defensive team must decide which half-court attack to employ. It does not necessarily hold that the defensive pattern established in back court should prevail in front court. In other words, a team might decide to utilize the full-court man-to-man pressure in back court and switch to the front-court zone after the trap is broken.

By this time it should be obvious that an effective full-court pressure trap defense must be an integral phase of the defensive repertoire used by teams that employ mid-court traps. Full-court trapping is a rather broad, complicated topic and time does not permit the discussion of that phase of the defensive game. It is only necessary to mention that the effectiveness of half-court traps will vary proportionately to the diversity of attacks used by the defensive team, providing all other elements are anywhere near equal.

Half-court Traps

Man-to-Man. If an offensive team can effectively break full-court pressure defenses and knows how to fast break and score with consistency when they cut off defensive players, it is wise to use only half-court pressure traps. The defensive team merely retreats to mid-court and employs pressure and channelling tactics.

The major difference in starting the pressure at mid-court is the ball handler has more time to find an open man and pass the ball before he can be channelled into a trap. In other words, channelling the ball handler into a trap becomes very difficult.

It is also difficult for the defensive players guarding someone other than the ball handler to prevent their offensive men from either getting open or pulling them out of possible trap and intercept positions. In this case it is sometimes advisable to channel the ball to the corners away from mid-court to spring the trap. This can best be achieved by forcing the ball handler to pass the ball to the corner and adjusting the defense while the pass is in the air. Diagram 4 indicates how X3 and X4 are not closely guarding their men but inviting O1 to pass to O4.

While the ball is on the way from O1 to O4, X4 and X3 spring for the trap. X1 falls back sharply to handle the outlet pass to O1 or O2. X2 collapses to the foul-line area and O5 falls in to protect the basket. X1 and X2 become the primary interceptors, while X5 must concentrate on protecting the basket and preventing an offensive player from slipping in under the basket.

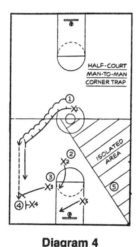

Diagram 4

NOTE: If the trap is broken, there must be a hurried reassignment of men. Each defensive man must know whom he is to cover and make a call to this effect. Talking on defense is imperative at this point. After considerable repetition, teammates will recognize switches and be able to anticipate cut-off routes necessary to intercept their new offensive player.

After several traps have been broken and the offensive team is still in control of the ball and the situation, the defensive team must not be disturbed but must continue their pressure to drive the ball to the closest corner for a trap. Persistence pays off here.

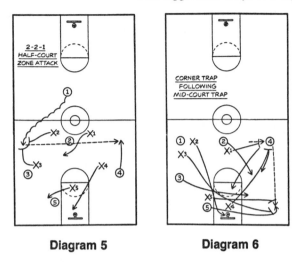

Diagram 5   **Diagram 6**

Zone. In Diagram 5 the defensive team is deployed in a 2-2-1 half-court alignment. However, this alignment will not hold true when the offensive team realigns its players.

O1 has the ball and dribbles across mid-court. X2 and X3 channel O1 to the mid-court corner, while X1 and X5 are maneuvering to intercept positions. X4 sprints back for protection of the basket. If O2 breaks the trap by passing to O4, X1 and X4 must activate the trap on O4, and X2, X3, and X5 must spring to the same positions on the opposite side of the floor. There is a small time lag here; however, the simplicity of teaching will outweigh this disadvantage. The best place for the offensive team to throw the release is the deep corner. Diagram 6 illustrates how the deep-corner trap is executed following the breaking of the mid-court trap.

X3 is the key. He must charge O5 cautiously for a cut-off position, forcing O5 back into the court, where X5 can complete his trap. X2 must move with the ball and take X3's place as protector of the basket. X4 and X1 collapse while the ball is in the air to become interceptors or "gap shooters."

Playing Your Own Game

There are many variations of these two basic trapping structures. Nevertheless, the success of any attack will depend upon the aggressiveness of the defensive team and how they vary their attack. The defensive team cannot allow the opponent to become familiar with either the structure or the tempo of the attack. Constant pressure and harassment of the ball handler will keep his head down and prevent him from making accurate passes which damage the floor positions of the defensive interceptors and trappers.

A trapping team must bear in mind that the opponent will occasionally get wide open shots. They must not panic when this happens. The offensive team will make many elementary mistakes which give the easy baskets back to the defensive team.

These two events will balance out on the average night. The important factor for the defensive team to remember is how well they execute the basic traps and handle the predicted offensive maneuvers. A basic breakdown in floor coverage, which can be attributed to lack of hustle, will damage the defensive team far more than the occasional superior play by the offensive team.

When the offensive team can consistently execute the superior play, they are probably going to win the game anyway. By employing the trap defense, a team is at least controlling their own destiny and getting beat doing what they want to do, rather than allowing their opponents to choose the weapon.

Great teams only become great because they master the techniques that allow them to control all phases of the game. The team that has the poise and finesse to completely control the tempo of the game did not acquire this ability over night. It takes many long, hard practice hours to master defensive techniques because the offensive team has the ball advantage.

Total Commitment

The most important factor each player must remember when executing trapping defenses is that gambling and taking chances are a must. Trapping defensive players cannot play it safe. They must gamble for the interception and steal.

There is no such thing as a safe trapping defense. The very essence of trapping defenses is the element of gamble. Players must learn how to gamble, even on their retreat or regroup movements.

The idea of constantly gambling is very hard to master. Most players have been trained to play safe, sound defense, and they are reluctant to throw caution to the winds and take too many chances.

NOTE: The ultimate success of the trap defense will depend upon all players completely committing themselves to gambling and risking all for an interception.

To steal or not to steal becomes the question. The team that consistently steals or intercepts the ball will successfully employ the trap defense.

13

Stunting Defenses in Basketball

by Buddy Comer

Head Basketball Coach
Page County High School
Shenandoah, Virginia

Buddy Comer has been coaching high school basketball for six years and has an overall won-lost record of 92-23. During that time his teams have won two regular-season district championships, one regional, and one state championship.

I have taken a cue from football in coaching defense. Football coaches stunt their defenses to confuse the offense and give the defense many looks; this has been my philosophy in coaching defense in basketball.

NOTE: With improved coaching techniques and player abilities at all levels, it is getting harder and harder to set up in one defense and expect to keep the offense from scoring at will.

But by changing or stunting defenses at different times or in the middle of patterns of play sequences, we have been able to break up the offensive patterns of many opponents.

Man-to-Man Defensive Fundamentals

Being a firm believer in a pressure type of man-to-man defense, I feel that man-to-man defensive fundamentals must be mastered before any type of defense will be effective.

NOTE: Thus, man-to-man fundamentals and drills are stressed throughout our entire program.

1-3-1 Match-Up Zone

The second type of defense that we use in our stunting schemes is the 1-3-1 match-up zone. In our man-to-man defense we will pressure all passing outlets on the ballside and slough and float on the weak or off side, trying to get as much weakside help as we can (Diagram 1).

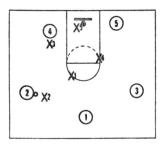 

Diagram 1   **Diagram 2**

By sloughing and using zone principles away from the ball, our man-to-man takes on a zone look and in many instances we are able to blend our 1-3-1 match-up zone without the offense realizing that we have gone into a zone.

In our program we try to spend at least 65% of all practice sessions on some phase of defense. We like to drop into a match-up zone and rotate to match the offensive alignment (Diagram 2). We like to rotate clockwise to make the match-up. We use our short or quick forward to play the 2 spot—so that when the rotation takes place we have a forward near the basket.

NOTE: Once we are matched-up with the offense we will stunt into various other defenses or variations of defense.

Various Keys

We stunt or change defenses by the use of various keys, which may be verbal or predetermined. One of the verbal keys is a live color called by a member of the defense. We always let the 5 man in our 1-3-1 match-up call the verbal keys. (We like to stunt from the match-up into our man-to-man defense.)

> **NOTE: The 5 man waits to see that every man has matched up; then he makes a color call and immediately every man takes the player in his area man-to-man and stays man-to-man until the next time down the floor. We let the back man, 5, give the key because he is in the best position to see the entire floor and can tell when everyone is matched-up.**

By starting in a zone defense and going to the man-to-man, we hope to create doubt in the offense's mind as to what defense we're in and what offense they must use. The back man uses many color calls during the game but only predetermined "live" colors mean anything.

This year we used red as our live color for stunting into man-to-man. Scouting tells us how much man-to-man to play against a particular team. Scouting will also help in the procedure to be used for matching-up. Another stunt that we use is to stunt to a straight zone from the match-up. Again, we use a verbal key—we usually stunt to the straight 1-3-1.

We also have some automatic or predetermined keys that we use to change defenses. We use a 2-3 defense on throw-ins from under the basket. I feel that this cuts down on the screens and pick-offs and eliminates many easy baskets. If the ball is lobbed back we immediately go to our match-up—then we are ready for our stunt to the man-to-man.

Trap Corners

Another stunt that we use is to trap corners any time that the ball is dribbled to the corner (Diagram 3). If the ball escapes the trap, we immediately go to our match up defense (in our case, the 1-3-1 match-up).

The 1-3-1 match-up also lends itself to a half-court trap defense. We key this part of our defense by the use of a predetermined key. This past year, we went to the trap any time the ball was taken out in the back court on the sideline.

Zone Pressing Advantage

Since we zone-pressed 100% of the time, we found that it was a big advantage to drop back into a match up zone and pick up men in areas. It seems extremely hard for high school players to pick up in a man-to-man

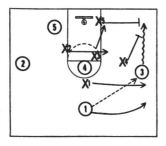

Diagram 3

from a zone press. We found that we gave up fewer easy baskets and still were able to stunt to the man-to-man defense.

> **NOTE: We huddled on foul shots this past year and were able to save time-outs and also were able to relay messages to the team. At this time we also changed defenses.**

Teaching Stunting Defenses

To be able to stunt effectively, you must start early in your practices to work on stunting and changing defenses. You must practice stunting daily. If your practice time does not allow for actual practice in changing defenses, your team will not be disciplined enough to be effective. Here are a few points to remember when teaching stunting defenses.

1. Start working on stunting early in your practice sessions.
2. Stunt from zone to man-to-man or from one zone to another. It is difficult to stunt from man-to-man to zone in the middle of a pattern.
3. Make sure that everyone is familiar with all defenses to be used.
4. Develop a simple numbering and/or color scheme for keys.
5. Work with the back man on defense so that he can recognize the right time to use the zone to man-to-man stunt.
6. Master man-to-man techniques and fundamentals.
7. Have skull sessions to explain stunting procedures.
8. Use handout materials with information and methods to be used on stunting.
9. Give your players a test periodically (written) to make certain that all of them know their assignments.
10. Work, work, work—it takes patience, patience, patience.
11. Use scouting reports so that you may use your stunts effectively. Scouting reports will help also in match up principles.
12. Use your strongest defense the largest portion of the time.

Conclusion

Our players enjoyed trying to fool the other team and worked quite hard and took pride in eliminating mistakes. In the tournament games we played, en route to winning the state championship, no team was able to shoot over 29% from the floor.

NOTE: We like to think that this was largely due to the indecision caused by our stunting defenses.

Our players were of average intelligence and had no problem adjusting to the changing and stunting defenses. I think that this was due to our working constantly in practice on mental discipline and on this phase of defense.

This type of defensive strategy is particularly effective against pattern teams that use different offenses for man-to-man and zone defenses. I have found that if a team is not well disciplined and poised, this type of defensive play will usually wreck its offense.

Part III

Conditioning and Drills

1

An All-Purpose Fundamental Drill

by Larry Taylor

Head Basketball Coach
Berry College
Mount Berry, Georgia

Larry Taylor played high school and college basketball be-
fore turning to coaching the game in 1959. As head basketball
coach at Berry College he has built an impressive record after
a short rebuilding program. His last three seasons were most
impressive: 18-7; 19-8; 20-8.

In our efforts to install an offense and a defense, we basketball coaches
often become so time-conscious that we neglect the elementary parts of
the game.

ALL-PURPOSE DRILL: In order to work on the basic
movements of the game, yet keep up the tempo of practice,
I decided to combine the fundamentals listed below into an
all-purpose drill (Diagram 1).

This fundamental drill includes the following basketball movements:

1. Faking with the ball—head and shoulder fakes both right and left,
rocker step. Check for overstepping on fakes, body leaning too far forward on fakes, and dragging pivot foot while faking.

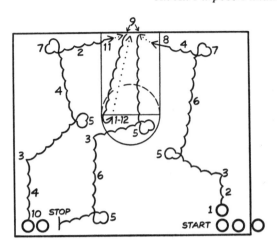

Diagram 1

2. Right-hand dribble—staying low on the dribble, and seeing that the fingers are cupped and in a relaxed state.

3. Change-direction dribble—dribble is pushed across extended front foot, a stagger step may be necessary to properly execute this maneuver.

4. Left-hand dribble—check for the same things as in no. 2.

5. Reverse dribble—stay low on the reverse movement, keep feet wide for good balance.

6. Change-of-pace dribble—be sure balance is good so that escalation of speed is smooth.

7. Reverse dribble on base line—same principles as in no. 5.

8. Glide lay-up shot—check for balance, a long step, and keeping the body between the ball and the basket. This is usually a bank shot.

9. Rebound and drive out—rebound his own lay-up and drive out; congestion of the area will make the player drive to an open hole.

10. Pivoting—reverse pivot and the forward or front pivot; check for proper balance, pivot foot staying wide for balanced landing, and protecting the ball while pivoting.

11. Fake and lay-up shot—drive to the basket, fake up with the ball before shooting the lay-up. Be sure the person faking does not hop or drag his pivot foot while executing the fake.

12. Jump shot from top of the key—the player rebounds the ball and drives to the foul lane where he executes a fake and then turns and shoots a jump shot.

PRACTICE TIPS: We spend approximately three minutes each day on this drill, and this enables each boy to work through the drill three times on each end of the floor. We

usually try to have a squad of 15 to 20 players. We spot check the players and insist that the drill be run at full speed with proper execution—and that they run the drill as diagrammed, which will eliminate any collision between players.

Execution: The players will start the drill on the right side of the court. This allows one group to start with the right-hand dribble and the other group to start with the left. All players waiting to begin should be working on faking or pivoting. As soon as a player gets to the "change-of-pace area" another player should start the drill. This will allow proper spacing between the players, and it is possible to have as many as seven or eight players on the same end of the court running through the drill.

NOTE: While this drill will not eliminate the need to work on additional drills, it should help solve the time factor in your practices.

2

Drills for Conditioning and Fundamentals

by Leslie Carrillo

Former Head Basketball Coach
Utterback Junior High School
Tucson, Arizona

Over the past seven years, Leslie Carrillo's basketball teams at Utterback Junior High School have a record of 79-44. Coach Carrillo has also coached for the last two years in Tucson's CYO Catholic Church League, composed of 12 teams of high school juniors and seniors. His 1967 CYO team won the league championship game and ended the season with a 15-2 record. In 1968 his team finished first in the league, winning 18 of their 20 games. Mr. Carrillo has retired from coaching and is presently House Administrator at Cholla High School (Cholla, Arizona).

Described here are some of the drills we have found most effective in conditioning our players and teaching them the fundamental skills of basketball. These drills have been derived from various sources and several will probably be familiar to you. Others may be new and useful. You may be able to adapt them, as I have done, to your particular needs and personnel.

NOTE: Though we like to use the same basic approach each year, we remain receptive to new ideas, changing

drills, and adding new ones each season. We are always trying to perfect our drills to help us accomplish our basic game objectives.

Drills and Game Philosophy

Setting the tempo: Our basic game approach centers on our belief that we must set the tempo of the game. We are out there to win and to win in our own way if possible. We want the other team to make mistakes, and we want to make fewer of them. The only way to accomplish these goals is to force the opponents to play our game.

We are prepared to run and press whenever necessary, usually from the start and throughout the game, but varying our speed. We run for a while, slow down for a while, run again, slow down again. To set this changing tempo, we must be in tiptop shape. Thus we begin on the very first day to condition ourselves both mentally and physically for the fast-running game. All of our drills and practices are geared to this idea of setting game tempo.

Defensive fundamentals: A second point of our philosophy which our drills are designed to effect is that a team must be sound in fundamentals, particularly the fundamentals of defense. We feel that defense is the *most* important aspect of the game. A good or even an excellent offensive pattern is worth little if you cannot get your hands on the ball more than the other team.

In our games we use a basic zone defense with man-to-man principles: If a man is in your zone, play him man-for-man until he leaves your zone. If you are overloaded in your zone, play the man closest to the ball. If there is no one in your zone, cheat to the ball side of the court. As soon as your team steals the ball, be ready to *run*.

All-Purpose Drills

Following are three drills we find effective in teaching a variety of basic skills and in conditioning our players.

Running Drill: The first of these all-purpose drills we call the Running Drill (Diagram 1). This incorporates four basic fundamentals, dribbling, passing, shooting lay-ups, and rebounding, all run at full speed. Running at full speed is essential when a team uses the fast break as we do.

To begin this drill, we have the boys line up on the baseline in two lines, side by side, facing the far basket. The player in line A dribbles with the ball up to about mid-court and then passes to the player in line B.

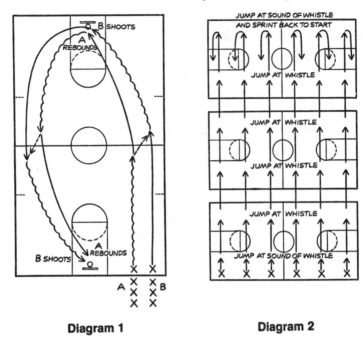

Diagram 1   **Diagram 2**

Player B dribbles the remaining distance to the basket for the lay-up. Player A rebounds and repeats as before, returning downcourt to the near basket. Each boy then changes lines.

Kangaroo Jump: To teach reactions to the ball overhead from the defensive stance, we use a drill called the Kangaroo Jump (Diagram 2).

> **USES: This drill is good for conditioning and developing jumping ability, quick reactions to a shooter, and reacting to the fast break from a defensive stance.**

Since we practice outdoors, we are able to use three courts lined up side by side for this drill, starting the drill at the sideline of the first court. The players are placed side by side the length of the court with their backs toward the inside of the court. Each boy assumes a good defensive position: semi-crouched, feet shoulder-width apart, one hand up and to one side and the other down and to one side, weight forward, and head looking straight ahead.

At the sound of a whistle the boys begin to backpedal, boxer style, until they hear a second whistle, at which time they stop backpedaling and jump up as high as they can, reaching as high as possible with both hands. They continue jumping until the whistle blows again, then begin to backpedal. This alternating procedure is continued until they reach the end of the last court, when I give a few quick spurts on the whistle. Then the boys *must* sprint back to the starting point.

NOTE: After about a minute's rest, we begin again, repeating this drill at least two more times, more if we feel we need conditioning. We also add slight variations by blowing the whistle in short spurts to make the boys return to the start from their backpedaling.

Circle Fast-break Drill: Another drill we use especially to coach the fast break from defense is what we call the Circle Fast-Break Drill (Diagram 3). In this drill we line up the boys inside the free-throw circle; two are placed side by side closest to the basket, three behind the two, all of them facing the basket. A manager or the coach throws the ball against the backboard and the closest boy grabs the ball and quickly turns to start the fast break.

The two outside back men take the fast-break lanes to the outside of the court, the middle man goes directly down the middle, and the remaining two trail, filling the remaining spaces on either side. Thus, what we have is basically a three-lane fast break with two trailers. Since we like to have the ball go down the middle as quickly as possible, the boy grabbing the rebound must look quickly to the middle to feed the man there. Then all five must sprint to the other basket and work for the shot.

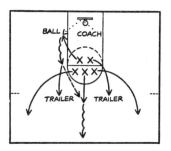

Diagram 3

VARIATIONS: A variation of this drill once players have gotten used to feeding the ball to the middle and filling the proper lanes, is to have them line up facing away from the basket and proceed as usual. Later on, feeding quickly to the outside and then to the middle can be incorporated. This is closer to game conditions when we must clear the free-throw lane first, then break down the middle.

We also like to vary the drill by having the rebounder fill the lead lane, be it the middle or one of the outside lanes. Finally, we attempt to use it in controlled-type scrimmages with two full teams, but only after they have mastered the moves.

Drills in Defensive Fundamentals

As stated previously, we believe that defense is the *most* important aspect of basketball. Here are some of the drills we find most effective in teaching basic defensive skills.

"Olé" Drill: The Olé Drill (Diagram 4) gets its name from my observations of some high school players allowing the offensive man to out-drive them going down the side and baselines with the ball. To me, these players look like bullfighters doing beautiful "derechazos," opening the gate for the man with the ball—hence the "Olé." When one of our boys does this, we all let him know it by giving him a loud clap for his terrific "cape work."

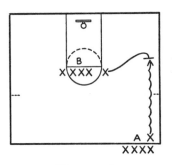

Diagram 4

We use the Olé Drill to help prevent our boys from being out-driven, starting the drill by placing one group at mid-court in a straight line facing the baseline, and a second group at the free-throw line facing the sideline. Then we proceed to work on a 1-on-1 situation. A player from Group A starts to dribble down the sideline in a straight line. Player B must then hustle to get in front of the man with the ball and cut him off.

With the rule making the offensive man equally responsible for contact in a charging situation, the defensive man has every right to be there. This move is perfectly legal providing the defensive man gives him just enough room.

> **NOTE: The most important thing to keep in mind is that the defensive man must keep his hands in a legal guarding position and not let his arms go straight to the side. If his arms moved to the side, the position would not be a normal**

guarding position and the defensive man would then be responsible for contact should any occur.

We work the Olé Drill on both sides and down the middle as we progress, but keep it simple at first by not allowing the A players to deviate from their straight-line path. Once the B men have mastered stopping the offensive man's progress, we then allow the offensive man to move to whichever side he wants to lose his defensive man. The defensive man's responsibility then rests on staying between his man and the basket at all times and forcing the offensive man to the outside. In this way the offensive man is hampered and limited in his opportunities to feed off the ball in actual game conditions, since he can only feed to the middle if he is forced to move to the outside.

As you can see, this drill has a twofold purpose. It allows us to work both offensively and defensively strictly in accord with my ideas: While on defense, force the dribbler to the outside; while on offense, work the ball to the middle. In its more advanced forms, we use it to get our boys on offense to fight the outside pressure and work the ball toward the sideline. At the same time, the boys get defensive work on forcing the offense to the outside with pressure.

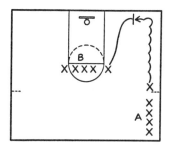

Diagram 5

BASE LINE DRILL: Our Baseline Drill (Diagram 5) is similar to the Olé Drill except that we do not want the offensive man to out-drive us down the baseline and under the basket for the easy lay-up. We let him turn the corner and then step in front to stop his progress.

Tandem Drill: The Tandem Drill is another defensive drill and even more, a game-conditioning drill. We work this drill by putting the defensive boys in 3-on-1, 3-on-2, and 3-on-3 situations as illustrated in Diagram 6. On the 3-on-1 the lead player must react to the ball and stop that man's progress, and go with each pass in an attempt to steal the ball. In the 3-on-2 situation, the lead or point man takes the middle man, the second man goes to the wing with the ball, and then the point man splits the difference between the ball and the nearest man. In the 3-on-3, the point man takes the middle man, the number 2 man takes the man who receives the pass, and the number 3 man goes to the opposite wing.

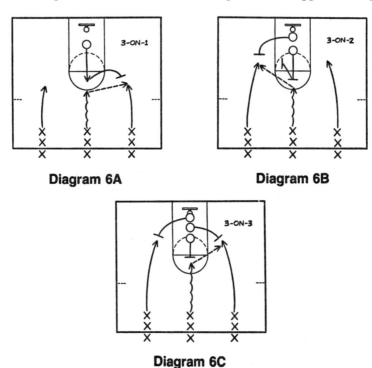

Diagram 6A   **Diagram 6B**

Diagram 6C

3

A Combination Rebound–
Fast-Break Drill

by Jim Hall

Head Basketball Coach
Senior High School
Dexter, Missouri

*Jim Hall's nine-year record at Dexter is 172 wins against 70
losses. His squads have been among the final eight teams in
the state tournament twice in the last four years.*

One of our basic beliefs about basketball is that no one can be a
consistent winner without good rebounding. Therefore, our regular
squads work very hard on rebounding fundamentals. Because we have
never been fortunate enough to have a good big player who could control
the boards primarily through his height, we spend a lot of time on technique.

**NOTE: This article will cover one of our best rebounding
drills. The main reason we use this specific drill is that it is
much more than just another drill for rebounding.**

This drill starts out as a rebounding drill and winds up as a fast-break
drill with the outlet pass, the filling of the lanes, and the attacking of
different combinations at the offensive end. Additionally, it serves as a
great conditioner early in the practice season. We run it at least twice a
week before game competition begins and once a week after the season

has started. Finally, one of the major features of this drill is that it allows the squad to work on several fundamentals in a supervised, game-like situation.

> **TECHNIQUE: No attempt will be made in this article to advocate any particular fundamental technique such as style of blocking off on rebounds or method of filling the lanes. Each coach can apply his own methods.**

The Drill

Initial stage: The beginning stage of the drill is shown in Diagram 1. The offensive players are placed in a balanced floor alignment with the two forwards about ten feet off the free-throw lane, the center just above the free-throw line, and the guards just outside the circle. The five defensive players are placed in the positions they would normally assume, and the head coach stands at the baseline where he can watch the action that develops.

We allow any one of the offensive players to shoot the ball to begin the drill. The player shooting the ball is asked to shoot a soft, natural shot, trying to *miss* the basket, but coming as close as he can—should he make the shot, he tries again.

> **NOTE: Since our basic defense is a sinking man-to-man, the defensive team must adjust its position somewhat, depending on which offensive player is taking the shot.**

Rebounding: As the shot is taken, all five offensive players try to go to the boards to gain offensive rebound position, while the defensive team uses its regular techniques to block off the offense. From the baseline, the coach can see whether the boys are doing what they are supposed to do both offensively and defensively.

> **FREEZE: When I want to emphasize or point out something, I simply blow the whistle as an indication that all the players are to freeze in position. At this time, everyone can see who blocked out his man correctly and who let his man get offensive position.**

To make it a real challenge, we encourage the offense as much as the defense. If the offense gains the rebound, they attempt to score—if they are in position to do so. If not, then we set up and run the drill again.

Fast break: The fast-break part of the drill begins as soon as the defense secures the rebound. Basically, what we try to do, as in Diagram

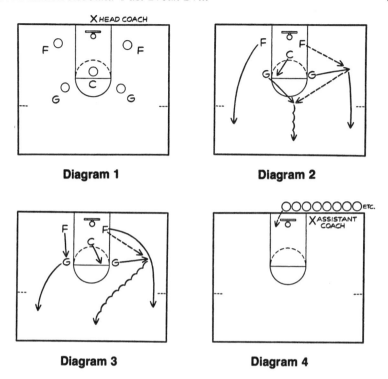

Diagram 1 **Diagram 2**

Diagram 3 **Diagram 4**

2, is get the ball out to the guard on the side the rebound came off, having the other guard fill the middle with the offside forward taking the outside lane. The other two front-line men serve as trailers.

Any time the guard gets the ball and feels that it would be advantageous to take it down the middle himself, he does so; and the other guard fills an outside lane (Diagram 3).

Opposition: We feel that the uniqueness of this drill comes as the ball reaches mid-court: the Junior Varsity squad and their coach now become involved in the drill by furnishing opposition at the offensive end of the floor. The squad is lined up as shown in Diagram 4 and, just before the teams rebound each time, the assistant coach will tell them how many will go out to play defense—one, two, or three will move out at any one time.

As the fast break reaches the mid-court area, the predetermined number of defensive (J.V.) players quickly assumes the proper position on the floor. The defense will create either a 3-on-1 (Diagram 5a), a 3-on-2 (Diagram 5b) or a 3-on-3 (Diagram 5c), depending on how many men the assistant coach has told to go out.

> **PURPOSE: This is done so that the offense doesn't know what kind of defensive situation they are going to face until the last minute. This way they will learn how to react to almost any situation.**

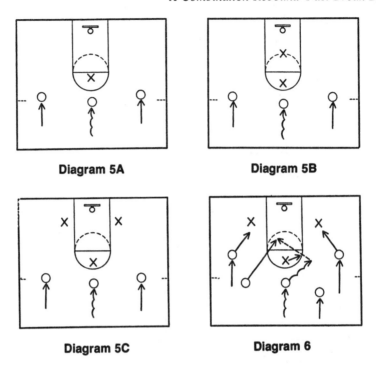

Diagram 5A   Diagram 5B

Diagram 5C   Diagram 6

Reaction of offense: The offense will have to react quickly and differently to each defensive alignment. The proper attack for a 3-on-1, 3-on-2, or 3-on-3 situation would vary with the philosophy of the coach. The one thing I try to impress on my squad is that any time we have a 3-on-1 or a 3-on-2 advantage and don't shoot a lay-up, we are giving the opposition a break—the last thing we want is a 5- to 10-foot jump shot.

3-on-3: In a 3-on-3 situation (Diagram 6), we have the guard in the middle with the ball clear to one side of the head of the circle and break the opposite trailer through for a lay-up.

Use: We normally run this drill for ten minutes during a practice session. The team that rebounded and went down on the fast break comes back down the court at half-speed and goes on offense. The other five go on defense and run the drill. However, any time a group goes down and doesn't attack the defense correctly, they must come back and go through the entire drill again.

Summary: We feel that this is one of our better drills. It teaches a great many fundamentals of the game and is an excellent conditioner. This drill offers a game-type, competitive situation in which everyone can observe what each person is doing.

4

An All-Purpose Offensive/ Defensive Drill

by Fred B. Yanero

Head Basketball Coach
Milford Mill Senior High School
Baltimore, Maryland

Fred Yanero has been coaching high school basketball for the last ten years–two years as junior varsity coach at Ashtabula High School (Ohio) where he posted a 25-10 record and eight years as head coach at Dundalk High School (Baltimore, Maryland) where his record was 122-29. At present, he is athletic director at Milford Mill Senior High School.

Every basketball coach should have a broad philosophy which covers all facets of the game as it concerns the development and improvement of not only the team, but also the individual player. I believe that his philosophy must encompass four areas:

Defensive basketball
Offensive basketball
Individual player development
Team improvement

The development and success of the team are dependent upon the effectiveness of the various methods which the coach uses to express his philosophy to his players.

Theory through drills: One of the better means of communicating with the players is through the use of game situation drills. For example, since I believe that offensive basketball is a continual series of 1-on-1, 2-on-2, and 3-on-3 situations, I try to use drills that will develop skills appropriate to these situations—attempting to break the opponents' defense and force them to play us 1-on-1, 2-on-2, or 3-on-3. Our basic plan of attack is a controlled fast break.

> **NOTE: I do realize that if a fast break is unsuccessful, we must then set up the offense and run patterns designed to give us these desired situations. We try to do this through strongside and weakside offense.**

Sample Game Situation Drill

Following is one of the many game situation drills we use during the season. This example is more complete than most, covering both our offensive theory and development and our defensive development.

1. Organization: A minimum of twelve players (or more with the players alternating) in different colored scrimmage vests—3 red, 3 yellow, 3 blue, 3 green—are paired up according to position, as: first-string guard, forward and center; second-string guard, forward and center. One player from each group can be interchanged from time to time.

> **NOTE: This drill will help prepare a second-string player for that time during the course of the season when he may be called on to fill in.**

Players should be coached in the following skills before this drill is begun:

Defensive rebounding.
Outlet pass to start a fast-break (middle or side).
Filling lanes for a fast break.
Getting the ball to the middle.
Playing a tandem defense against a fast-breaking team.
Offensive rebounding.
Ball handling (such as head up when dribbling, speed dribbling, looking up court, etc.)
Individual defensive stance.
Offensive patterns (strong- and weakside).
Players on outside lanes are taught to cross under basket (second phase of a controlled break).

2. Procedure: Set up a team of 3 red players, 3 blue, 3 green, and 3 yellow (Diagram 1). The coach will direct the red and blue team to one end, the green and yellow to the other. The mid-court helper cannot enter the action until the ball is dribbled or passed over the mid-court line. Then, he must run and place a foot in the mid-court circle before helping out.

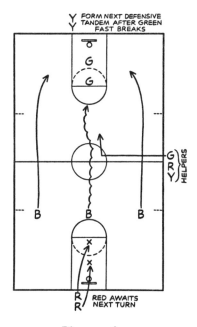

Diagram 1

> **INITIATING ACTION: Blue starts a break, with green set up in a defensive tandem at the end of the court. On gaining possession of the ball, green breaks against red.**

3. Defensive practice: Through the use of this drill, players should gain defensive practice in such skills as forming a defensive tandem to stop a fast break, individual defense and reaction, defensive rebounding, releasing and defensing against outlet passes, and fast breaking when a fast-break team scores.

Each player learns how to run our basic man-to-man defense and improve his stance, to call picks and jump from behind the pick to kill the dribbler. He learns to switch, to slide through the top, and to sag to the ball. Each defensive player has the opportunity to improve his ability to block off the offensive board and cut off the baseline, and the chance to work on defense pivot play and overplay.

4. Offensive practice: Our defensive players gain experience in the controlled fast-break through the use of this drill—which incorporates ball handling, shooting, and offensive rebounding—all under game conditions. They learn how to use the defensive rebound and the outlet pass as an offensive weapon. The rebounder learns to be a traveler or to fill the lane opposite the side he passed the ball out to. When a pass is to side-middle, the receiver learns to leap to the middle, giving the side passer a good target. Further, the middle man learns to drive to the foul line, and pass, shoot, or set up an offense.

> NOTE: If our fast-break is not successful, we must then run our offensive patterns. One day we may practice strongside options; another, we run through weakside options—if we believe our next opponent uses a zone, we work more on our weakside options.

Summary: A drill such as this has several distinct advantages. It involves all the players at one time and is an excellent conditioner. It develops poise, offensive and defensive techniques and the floor sense of each player, and helps the coach communicate and practice his controlled break philosophy.

> KEY POINT: The strongest part of this drill is the conditioning of the team to run offensive patterns when a fast-break is unsuccessful.

5

Fundamental Drills for High School Play

by F. F. Futch

Head Basketball Coach
Spearsville High School
Spearsville, Louisiana

Coach Futch has a 16 year record at Spearsville of 309 wins against 154 losses, and his teams have won six district titles.

It's our belief that fundamentals are all-important to the game of basketball. Players must master the fundamentals first if they are ever to master championship play.

NOTE: The player who does not grasp the value of skill in fundamentals not only hurts his team but himself as a player. We feel that you must build your offense and defense on a foundation of good fundamentals.

We have some favorite drills for mastering the fundamentals. They have done the job for us over the years and can very well help your program. First, I will give the fundamentals we stress and then the drills to perfect them.

Fundamentals

Receiving: The most important factor in catching or receiving the basketball is relaxation. You can't fight the ball. For example, I take a basketball and throw it hard against the wall and it comes back rapidly. Then I throw a basketball against the curtain on the stage and it falls softly.

> **NOTE: This is to show them you need to cushion the pass by moving the arms back toward the body with elbows slightly bent. Fingers and thumbs should be well spread and the player should always step forward to meet the pass to avoid interceptions. As in throwing a pass, a player must always keep his eye on the ball.**

Passing: We teach four types of passes and as in shooting we have a target to aim at—the receiver's chin. Most young players have a tendency to throw the ball too low, so we raise the target. The basic passes are as follows:

1. Two-hand chest pass: It can be thrown from any position and is an ideal short pass and medium-length pass to use in the fast-break. It is usually thrown from a stride position and we expect our guards to use it extensively. In most cases the knees are bent slightly and the body is forward a little. Elbows are close to the body and forearms nearly parallel to the floor.

> **TIPS: The ball is grasped firmly with the fingers and thumbs. Head is up so the player can survey as much of the playing area as possible. In releasing, the player steps forward with his front foot in the direction of the receiver.**

2. Overhead pass: All the mechanics are the same as the chest pass. This pass usually can be thrown without interference and resembles the two-hand overhead shot we used to see.

3. Bounce pass: This is used basically to get the ball to the pivot and is a good close-in pass. Throwing this pass, the right-handed player steps to the side with his right foot and retains body balance. The body weight is on the right leg which is bent at the knee. The ball should strike a point on the floor about 3 feet from the receiver and should bounce about belt high.

> **NOTE: At first, the boys will usually bounce it too close to the receiver.**

4. Baseball pass: The ball is carried with both hands to a position within 3 or 4 inches of the right ear. Weight is on the rear leg and as the pass is executed, the left hand is released. The last point of contact is the fingertips.

Dribbling: Dribble until that ball seems like an extension of your hand.

The basics are simple—head up to see where you are going; fingers spread; palm down and off the ball; knees slightly bent; keep the ball low. We stress dribbling for speed, dribbling for protection of the ball and dribbling for change of pace. We learn to dribble equally well with either hand.

Shooting: We spend about 30 minutes per day in shooting practice. Each boy has his own ball and he practices shooting from the place on the floor where he shoots the most during a game. We allow him to do this for 15 to 20 minutes and then we begin formal shooting drills.

Not too many players know what they are shooting at. We want them to shoot the ball softly just over the rim. We don't want them using the board except when they are on the side of the basket. A little backspin on the ball is good. We want the fingers spread, palm off the ball, eyes on the target, good spring in the legs as they go up—the index finger should be the last point of contact with the ball.

> **NOTE: Handling the unorthodox shooter is a common problem in high school basketball. We feel that if an unorthodox shooter hits a good percentage we shouldn't try to change him. But if he's not hitting a good percentage, we do change him.**

Fundamental Drills

Passing and receiving the ball

1. File passing: Line up players on each end of the court. First man in one line passes ball to first man in second line. Use this drill for hand-offs as well.

2. Figure 8 (full- and half-court): An old but effective drill. Man in middle starts by passing ball to either side and then going behind the man he passes to.

3. Baseball pass: Use two balls and two lines. Left line breaks and right line hits at center court with a baseball pass. Right line breaks and receives pass from left line and shoots lay-up. Left line rebounds.

4. Chest pass: Set up five lines as shown in Diagram 1. Line 1 passes to 2 and goes to end of that line; 2 passes to 3; 3 passes to 4; 4 passes to 5; 5 passes to 1. Maintain fast tempo.

Dribbling drills

1. Set up five lines: First man in each line makes two trips for speed; two for change of pace; two to receive pivot at center. Change direction on whistle.

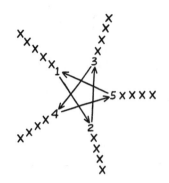

Diagram 1

Diagram 2

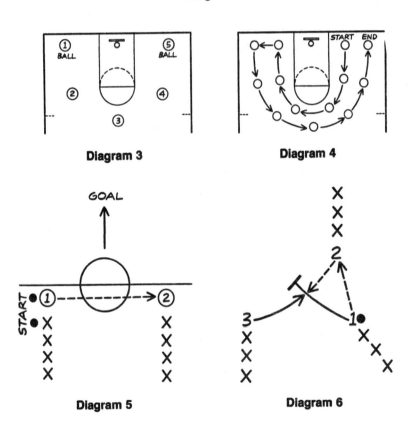

Diagram 3   **Diagram 4**

Diagram 5   **Diagram 6**

2. Tag: Give each of five men a ball and these five are "it"—rest of squad tries to avoid tag from the five men dribbling. If successful, the man touched becomes "it."

3. Dribble and turn: Line up five men at center of court (Diagram 2). The rest of the squad is divided on each side as shown. The first men on each side dribble in and around to first man past center and come back. The dribblers should pass the man in middle at same time.

Rebounding drills

1. One-on-one: Line up in pairs, back to back, at free-throw line with lid on the basket. As coach shoots, both men break for the basket and try to rebound.

2. Three men at basket: Man in middle throws ball against board, rebounds and passes to his left and goes to that position. This man dribbles to front of board, throws ball against board, rebounds, throws to man on his right and goes to that position. Drill continues in this manner.

Shooting drills

1. Lay-ups: Two lines shooting, right, then left, then down the middle.

2. Quick shot drill: Set up as shown in Diagram 3. Use two balls. The shooter takes a quick shot, retrieves the ball, throws to another man and moves to a different spot.

3. Around the world: Divide the squad into two groups with half on each end of the floor. Put better shooters on one end and poorer on the other to make competition even. First shooter starts under the basket and keeps shooting until he misses (Diagram 4). Rest of shooters take their turn. If you miss you go back to starting point.

4. Jump shooting: Form two lines at center with two balls (Diagram 5). Balls are in line 1. Line 1 passes to 2 at right side of free-throw lane and goes behind his screen; 1 receives ball from 2 and shoots jumper; 2 rebounds. Change lines.

5. Shooting behind screen: Set up as shown in Diagram 6. 1 passes to 2; breaks to right of free-throw lane and sets screen; 2 passes to 3 for shot.

6

Shooting Drills from the Percentage Areas

by Ralph Beeler

Head Basketball Coach
Bearden High School
Knoxville, Tennessee

Ralph Beeler has been coaching high school basketball since 1958–Maynardville High School (Maynardville, Tennessee), 1958-60: West Rome High School (West Rome, Georgia), 1960-65; Bearden High School, 1965-present–and has an overall record of 207-142. His 1971 team was runner-up in the district and advanced to the semi-finals of the regional tournament. Both his 1968 and 1972 teams placed fourth in the district, and his 1973 team placed third.

We try to have our players take their shots from the areas in which they can hit a high percentage. So during our shooting practice we control the area from where they shoot.

NOTE: We have definite areas from which to shoot in our man-to-man offense and definite areas to attack the zone defenses. We practice shooting for 30 minutes every day. Here are some of the things we do.

Around the world: For this drill we set up as shown in Diagram 1. We work our varsity and junior varsity together so we have 24 players drilling

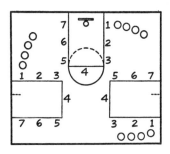

Diagram 1

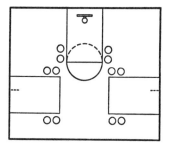

Diagram 2

at one time. We divide the squad so that we have four players at each bucket—and everyone has a basketball. We shoot from the seven spots indicated in the diagram for about five minutes.

> NOTE: Our boys shoot jump shots from these areas and use the backboard in areas 1, 2, 6, and 7. The shooting takes place simultaneously at all six buckets with the managers keeping time.

High Post: The next thing we do is shoot from the side high post. We line up with two men on each side with their backs to the bucket as shown in Diagram 2. We make them fake to the inside, pivot, face the bucket, and then take the jump shot. Next they fake outside, pivot, and take the jump shot.

> NOTE: After this, with their backs still to the bucket, we have them fake inside, take one dribble and take the jump shot. This is shown in Diagram 3. We execute this drill for about five minutes, alternating from the left side to the right side.

Pro: Our pro drill is shown in Diagram 4, with our players lined up on

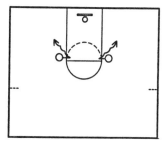

Diagram 3

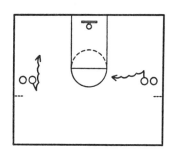

Diagram 4

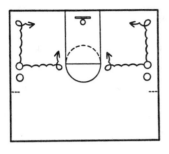 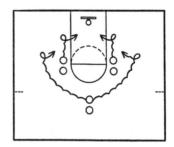

Diagram 5   **Diagram 6**

each side of the court at the wing position. Each player has a ball and imagines he has a man in front of him. He will fake right and go left taking two or three dribbles, pulling up and taking the jump shot—or he will fake left and go right taking two or three dribbles, pulling up for the jump shot. He then drives toward the baseline or the free-throw line. The drill is run for five minutes.

Reverse: The reverse drill is shown in Diagram 5. We line up as shown and drive toward the free-throw line—then do a reverse dribble and shoot a jump shot coming off the pivot. This is done from both sides. We also go toward the baseline and use a reverse dribble. In Diagram 6 we illustrate the reverse dribble from the high post and also from the point position.

> NOTE: At the high post we will dribble half way down the lane and do a reverse dribble into the 3-second lane. We do a lot of shooting in that area because we have found our players get several shots a game there.

At the point we drive toward the wing position and do a reverse dribble and shoot the jump shot coming off the reverse. We run this drill for about five minutes.

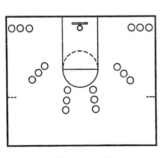 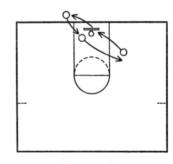

Diagram 7   **Diagram 8**

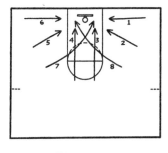 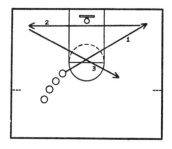

Diagram 9   **Diagram 10**

Quick shooting: For our quick-shooting drill we use the three areas on the floor shown in Diagram 7. We shoot out of the corner, on the side and out front. We are working on the one-hand push shot—and the players have to make a total of 11 goals from one area before they can move to another.

> NOTE: We alternate each day, going right side one day and left side the next. Using only one ball, we make them get their own rebound and throw it back to their line. We stress getting the shot off as quickly as possible.

Lay-ups: Next we shoot lay-ups at all six goals. At each goal three players run a figure 8 (Diagram 8) then shoot lay-ups from eight different directions as shown in Diagram 9.

> NOTE: This concludes our 30 minutes of shooting drills.

Specialty work: During our specialty time each day, we have the players tipping at each goal, using their left and right hands. We also have them do power lay-ups. This is going up and getting an offensive rebound and powering the ball back in the basket.

During the season we will subsitute other shooting drills for some of those mentioned, especially if we are playing a team that uses a zone. A drill we employ if we are playing against a 1-3-1 zone is shown in Diagram 10. We use only guards and forwards in this drill; the centers continue to work on shooting areas.

> EXECUTION: Following the pattern of shooting illustrated in Diagram 10, we go from left side to right corner; from right corner to left corner; from left corner to right side. We then reverse the action.

7

Free-Throw Drill

by Dennis Bridges

Head Basketball Coach
Illinois Wesleyan University
Bloomington, Illinois

Coach Bridges' eight-year record at Illinois Wesleyan is 131 wins against 78 losses. This includes four conference championships and three NAIA District 20 championships.

This drill is the only organized free-throw work that we do. Our players are urged to include some free-throw shooting practice in their pre-practice warm-up shooting. Along with some sort of required repetition free-throw shooting, a high school coach may want to use this drill.

Using the drill for the past four seasons, our composite free-throw percentage has been .712. But five seasons ago, my first at IWU, a conference champion and national tourney quarterfinalist team did not use the drill—and had a season mark of .629. The composite field-goal percentage over the past four years was the same as that of the first team, five years ago—44%. So I'm convinced that this drill has been the difference in free throwing. More important, I always feel that we are well prepared for that pressure free throw in the clutch.

Game-condition pressure shooting is the drill's outstanding feature, but also included as benefits are conditioning and team accomplishment.

TIP: This drill should be used only at the end of practice: it can be very tiring, thus draining your players for further practice. We use it every day for our final work; we have had practices end with backslapping and handshakes when a player makes a clutch shot that singals "showers" for the squad.

Line your squad along the endline. On the whistle have them sprint to touch the free-throw line (or free-throw line extended) and back to touch the end-line. Without stopping they sprint to touch the ten-second line and back to touch the endline. Still without stopping they sprint the length of the court to touch the other endline and return.

Using a ten-man squad as an example: as soon as the squad has run this course, call any five players out to shoot one free-throw each.

REPEAT: Repeat the run again; then the first five shooters again shoot one free throw each; again repeat the run; then the second five shooters take one free throw each.

Each night before the drill begins, make it clear to the boys what the goal is to shower. We always start at 70%—in this case (ten players) 14 out of 20. If the goal is not achieved, we go down one to 13 of 20 and run the drill again. Again if not achieved, we go down another to 12 of 20 and run the drill again. So it goes until finally the goal is met.

Experience using this drill has taught:

1. Make sure that these are *sprints*. Allow no sitting down for the five men waiting while the others shoot.
2. Always insist that the goal be reached, no matter how low you choose to go. You protect yourself from "all night" running by lowering the goal by one each time. As a matter of pride we never lower below 50%.
3. You may include a "bonus" chance to shower by agreeing that if all in one group of five make their shots, everyone showers.
4. If you are looking for a night of extra running, set the first goal above 70%. We never start below that figure.
5. A large group is too unwieldy—fourteen or fifteen men is a maximum. If you have a large squad, split into two groups. If you have full courts running each way, run cross-court and shoot at each end. Each end is governed by its own goal. If you don't have full cross-courts, run together but shoot at each end and again have each end governed only by its goal.

6. The drill is adaptable to practice needs. Run the varsity cross-court at one end and shower early. Half court scrimmage the B squad at the other end.

7. Keep the boys informed as to how they're doing. For example: three of five made, coach says, "You need 11 of 15 to shower."

8

A Fast-Break Fill-In Drill

by Richard Harvey

Head Basketball Coach
Kenmore West High School
Tonawanda, New York

Richard Harvey has been head basketball coach at Kenmore West High School since 1966 and has an overall record there of 110 wins, 36 losses. This includes an AAA Sectional championship (1967), unprecedented five-straight league championships (1968-69, 1969-70, 1970-71, 1971-72, 1972-73), and runner-up in the AAA sectional play-offs (1972). His squads have qualified for post-season sectional play the last eight years. Coach Harvey has authored a book, "Coaching Basketball's Multiple-Set Zone Offense" Parker Publishing Company, West Nyack, New York, and in 1973, he was selected Coach-of-the-Year of Western New York by Sports Digest.

Through experience I have found that most fast-break drills revolve around a continuous repetition of a specific situation. Examples of this type of drill would include—the continuous 3-on-2 break; the continuous 2-on-1 break; the traditional 3-man weave; the 3-man lane attack; other variations of the weave.

NOTE: Each of these drills has the obvious advantage of positioning the offensive players to take advantage of the uneven situation and eventually end up with a lay-up. However, the continuous repetition of a specific situation, although giving a player excellent knowledge in filling the lanes to spread the defense, does not afford the players enough experience in making mental adjustments to cope with varying fast-break situations.

Fast-Break Situations

Fast-break situations develop during a game as a result of a defensive rebound, a steal off a missed foul shot, jump ball plays, set patterns against presses, and out-of-bounds plays. To be successful, a team must be able to adjust and capitalize when these situations present themselves. Players have to learn to react both offensively and defensively.

DRILL: Therefore, I have attempted to create a fast-break drill which will include the various fast-break situations that normally occur in a game and incorporate them into a smooth-running continuous drill. The fast-break opportunities covered in the drill include the 2-on-1, 3-on-2, 4-on-3, 5-on-4, 3-on-1, and the 4-on-1.

Drill Setup

The drill is set up in the following manner.

Three players (ABC) form a cup around the basket to initiate a 3-man fast break off the rebound (Diagram 1). Two players (DE) are stationed at midcourt to defense the fast break as it develops. The rest of the team is positioned out-of-bounds at midcourt.

As the 3-on-2 fast break materializes, three things can happen that dictate the offensive and defensive adjustments to continue the drill:

1. The shot will be made by the offensive team.
2. The shot will be missed and rebounded by the defensive team.
3. The ball will be turned over to the defensive team without a shot being taken, because of:
   a. bad pass
   b. poor pass reception
   c. defensive steal

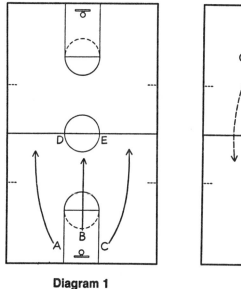
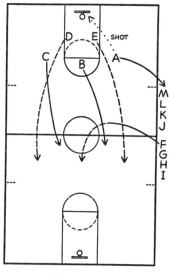

Diagram 1   **Diagram 2**

d. violation (called by coach)

e. offensive foul (called by coach).

NOTE: A foul may be committed by the defensive team. To save time, it is treated as a shot made.

Rules of Action

If the shot is made, the shooter moves off the court to the end of the line. The remaining players become the defense in the next fast-break situation.

EXAMPLE: Players ABC break against players DE. Player A makes the shot and moves off the court to the end of the line. Players BC remain on the floor to defense the next fast break. Player F joins players D and E to form a 3-on-2 break (Diagram 2).

If the shot is missed and a defensive rebound is secured, only the player missing the shot remains on the floor to defense the next fast break. The other players go to the end of the line.

EXAMPLE: Players ABC break against players D and E. Player A misses the shot and player D rebounds. Player A

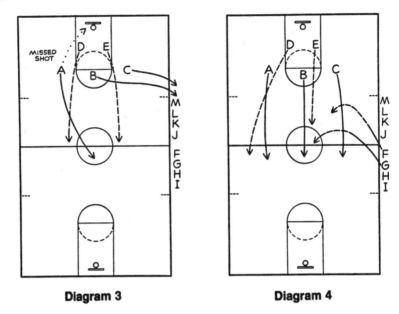

Diagram 3   Diagram 4

remains on the floor to defense players D and E in a 2-on-1 break (Diagram 3).

If the ball is turned over to the defense without a shooting attempt, all players remain on the floor to defense the next fast break.

> **EXAMPLE: Players ABC throw the ball away during the 3-on-2 break against D and E. Therefore players ABC remain on the floor to defense the next fast break. To compensate, players F and G join players D and E to create a 4-on-3 fast break (Diagram 4).**

The drill continues with the players filling in from midcourt to form the various fast-break situations. The offensive team always has one more player than the defense to form a fast-break situation. The only exceptions occur when a turnover happens in a 4-on-3 break or a 5-on-4 break. In these cases the resultant fast breaks are a 3-on-1 and a 4-on-1 respectively.

Situations and Adjustments

A breakdown illustration of the fast-break situations developing in the drill and the adjustments is shown in Chart I.

		Chart I		
		resulting fast-break situation		
		shot made	*shot missed*	*turnover*
3 on 2		3 on 2	2 on 1	4 on 3
2 on 1		2 on 1	2 on 1	3 on 2
4 on 3		4 on 3	3 on 1	5 on 4
3 on 1		3 on 2	2 on 1	4 on 3
4 on 1		4 on 3	2 on 1	5 on 4
5 on 4		5 on 4	4 on 1	5 on 4

Note: If a turnover results from a 5 on 4 break, a 5 on 4 remains by removing the shooter or the drill ends and starts over with a 3 on 2.

Possible Sequence

A final example of a possible sequence of fast-break situations is shown in Chart II.

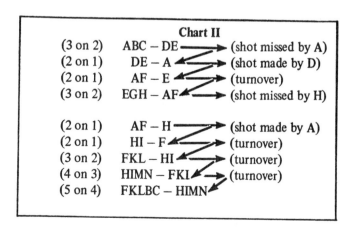

Chart II

(3 on 2)   ABC – DE ⟶ (shot missed by A)
(2 on 1)   DE – A ⟶ (shot made by D)
(2 on 1)   AF – E ⟶ (turnover)
(3 on 2)   EGH – AF ⟶ (shot missed by H)

(2 on 1)   AF – H ⟶ (shot made by A)
(2 on 1)   HI – F ⟶ (turnover)
(3 on 2)   FKL – HI ⟶ (turnover)
(4 on 3)   HIMN – FKL ⟶ (turnover)
(5 on 4)   FKLBC – HIMN

Conclusion

In conclusion the advantages of this fast-break drill are as follows.

1. Players must remain alert to the action on the floor.

2. Players must think and react to the changing situations and fill the necessary positions on the floor.

3. The drill relieves boredom which can be caused by a constant repetition of the same situation.

4. The drill places a premium on making the shot.

5. The fast-break situations normally occurring in a game will occur in this drill.

9

Circuit Training for Basketball

by William DuBois, Jr.

Head Basketball Coach
John A. Coleman High School
Kingston, New York

William DuBois' experience in basketball theory has been gained on both the high school and college levels. Returning to college in 1966 and graduating in 1968 at the age of 31, Coach DuBois began his coaching career at Ulster Community College where, while he was the assistant basketball coach, the basketball teams compiled a 45-9 record. In 1969 he became Director of Athletics and Head Basketball Coach at John A. Coleman High School in Kingston, New York. His first year as varsity pilot brought the first winning season ever achieved by a Coleman varsity basketball squad (12-6). This team received an invitation to an upstate Regional Catholic High School Tournaent—also a premier experience for a varsity squad. His overall record to date at Coleman is 70-38.

Why use circuit training? What is its value? Is it a better method of training than others? And if so, why? The answers to these questions—which I would like to share with other basketball coaches—I have found to be positive ones.

NOTE: Circuit training because it is quite flexible can be adapted to help any individual. Its primary use is to develop all-around muscular and circulo-respiratory efficiency.

Some Background

One's wind, a by-product created by the circulatory and respiratory systems, is dependent upon the heart, blood vessels and lungs. The lungs, which act as a storehouse for wind, take in oxygen and release carbon dioxide. Simultaneously, the circulatory system carries the gases to and from the muscles. The success of this biological process of breathing enables one to endure the strain caused by any type of physical activity.

The Program

In basketball, the athlete's maximum effort used in conditioning is best. However, this rigorous training cannot continue for any extended period. A break or "slower pace" exercise would act as a retarding process for the vital circulatory-respiratory organs.

As time passes in the circuit training program, time allotted to execute a certain number of exercises is increased from five minutes the first week, to seven minutes the second week, and ultimately to ten minutes the third week and afterwards.

After five minutes, the average athlete completes approximately one circuit and three exercises of the second one. After seven minutes, he completes approximately two circuits plus one exercise of the third circuit. And after ten minutes, usually the fourth week, each athlete should be able to complete three circuits.

NOTE: Thus, the trainee must push himself continuously throughout this program to meet the accelerated, required goals. Basketball, being a demanding sport, requires its players to be in top physical and mental condition if they are to give maximum effort. A player who does not achieve this standard cheats himself, his coach, and his team.

Initial Objective

Our initial objective is conditioning and this is where circuit training plays a paramount role. As stated, the time spent on a conditioning program is of primary importance. Our program lasts from three to four weeks and demands of its players strong legs, wrists, hands (especially the fingers), shoulders, and lower back. Consequently, a healthy circulo-respiratory system is of great importance in circuit training.

Techniques

Each coach must decide for himself the techniques he should use after surveying his facilities and personnel. Each athlete trying for maximum output is pre-tested to determine his maximum repetitions in one and one-fourth minutes, excluding push-ups.

These are done with no time limit involved as we want to get the athlete's maximum output. The coach records the pre-test score and if satisfied that each athlete performed at his peak, then divided each score by one-half—which in turn becomes the athlete's immediate goal.

Following the pre-test, each day the athlete should attempt to complete as many circuits as possible, using the new number of repetitions recommended by the coach. One circuit consists of each of the eight exercises (Diagram 1) described in our routine. Time allotted for this training after

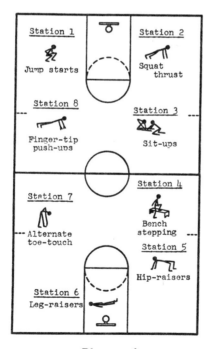

Diagram 1

the third week is ten continuous minutes without rest, thus pushing each athlete to his threshold of fatigue, and ultimately pain. Only through these rigorous requirements will circuit training meet its objective of increased strength and circulo-respiratory endurance.

> **NOTE: We have borrowed many training techniques from track and wrestling coaches. By varying these to suit our needs, we have developed our "Circuit Training for Basketball" program. This consists of eight exercises, each making its own contribution to the physical development of the player. The routine runs as follows:**

1. Jump Starts: In a crouch position, hands at your knees with feet shoulder-width apart, forcibly jump 8 to 12 feet high, swinging the arms above the head. As the body comes down on the balls of the feet, the arms and body swing into their original position and the exercise is repeated. Jump starts are used to strengthen muscles of the ankles, knees and hip extensors. Another exercise used to strengthen the ankles is to walk on the toes, the heels, the instep and on the outside of the foot.

2. Squat Thrust: Done to a four count. Starting position is at attention. On the count of 1, go into a squat position; count of 2, legs are together and thrust straight out to the back. On the count of 3, return to the squat position and on the count of 4, return to the original position of attention. The muscles developed in this exercise help develop the spine, hips, knees and ankles. Also, there is slight abdominal development.

3. Sit-Ups: Starting position is on the back with legs together straight out on the floor, and hands clasped behind the neck. A partner holds the legs at the ankles or just below the knee caps. Touch the right elbow to the left thigh, then return to the prone position. Next, touch the left elbow to the right thigh and again resume the original position. We have now completed one four-count repetition. Although a complete sit-up is usually counted each time the person returns to the lying position, in my program, one complete sit-up is when the four-count is finished.

4. Bench-Stepping: Place left foot on the bench, then bring the right foot up onto the bench next to the left foot. Lower the left foot and then the right foot. Repeat the same, raising the right foot first. The bench should be at least 12 inches high. Primarily, this develops the hip extensors, thighs, and knees.

5. Hip-Raisers: Starting position is sitting on the floor with feet flat on the floor approximately shoulder-width apart. Knees should point toward the chest. Arms and hands are directly behind the back with palms flat on the floor. On the count of 1, you push with arms and legs, raising the hips to shoulder level, throwing the head back. From a lateral view, this should resemble a table. On the count of 2, return to the original position. Primary development is for the erector muscles of the back and the extensors of the hips.

6. Leg-Raisers: Done to a four-count. Starting position is lying in the supine position, legs together, with arms at side. At the count of 1, you raise the legs no higher than 6 inches off the ground. On the count of 2, spread your legs; on the count of 3, close the legs. On the count of 4, resume the starting position. Primary development is for the thigh muscles and the abdominal wall.

7. Alternate Toe-Touch: Done to a four-count. Starting position is hands on hips, feet spread apart approximately shoulder width. On the count of 1, bend at the trunk of the body, touching your left hand to the right toe, then back to the starting position. Repeat, using the opposite hand and toe. We are now at the count of 3. On the count of 4, we are back at the original position, standing. Primary development is for the back and thigh.

8. Fingertip Push-Ups: Standard men's push-ups with back straight and arms extended are used with the exception of the hands. Ordinarily, the upper part of the body rests on the palms of the hands. However, I require my boys to use their fingertips. By developing the fingers, we get better ball control, essential in basketball. Primary development is for the chest, triceps of the arms and the shoulder muscles.

Conclusion

In addition to this routine, we require our athletes to run a two-mile course every other day beginning on Monday. Surprisingly enough, there is no physical evidence of routine output on running days when compared with non-running days.

NOTE: The biggest advantage in this type conditioning program is that it takes very little time, giving more time to the players and coach to work on fundamentals.

The exercises described in this article comprise but a small part of the John A. Coleman High School pre-training program for basketball conditioning, but serves to illustrate why we believe circuit training is a most valuable method of conditioning.

10

Ideas and Drills for Teaching Individual and Team Defense

by Charles G. Brehm

Head Basketball Coach
Fort Hays State College
Hays, Kansas

Chuck Brehm is in his ninth year as head basketball coach at Fort Hays State. During his high school and college coaching career, Brehm has compiled a 225-136 record including a Rocky Mountain Athletic Conference championship in 1970-71. He is also assistant professor in the division of health, physical education, and recreation. Coach Brehm came to FHS in 1965 after being named National Junior College Coach-of-the-Year at Dodge City Junior College. He posted a 113-29 mark at Dodge City through five years and led his team to the National Junior College championship in 1965.

Defensive basketball has always been a phase of the game that every coach would like to feel his team performs well. Achieving this goal is one of the most difficult tasks the coach faces at the beginning of the basketball season.

NOTE: We all have an idea of the style of defense we would like our teams to play—but many times the difference be-

tween good and average defense depends on player-coach communication.

Certainly, player-to-player communication is of vital importance in playing good defense, but in order for that player to understand how he is to play--player-coach communication is the first concern. Here are some ideas in this respect.

Basic Terminology

The past two seasons our team defense has improved because we have established some basic terminology to accompany our team defense. The fundamentals of individual defensive play have been discussed many times. The purpose of this article is not to rehash these fundamentals, but to discuss some terminology and drills that have helped improve our defensive game.

> **NOTE: The terminology is not unique to our particular style of basketball—but has been borrowed from many coaches throughout the country, principally Bob Knight, formerly of West Point and now at Indiana University.**

Head on the ball: This term deals with the stance of the defensive player. On the side- and baseline we like to play with our inside foot forward with the weight evenly distributed or slightly back, knees bent, hands up above the waist, and our target the offensive man's hips or his belt buckle.

The defensive man must always have his head directly between the ball and the basket. We are interested in position first rather than stealing the ball. Although we want the hands moving, we do not want to over-reach to the point that we forget to move our feet. If the offensive man goes to the right, we use the right hand. The back hand is used to pick up the cross-over dribble.

> **NOTE: In our early practice session, we will keep our hands behind our backs in order to concentrate on foot movement and keeping the head on the ball. Defense is played with the feet, and we emphasize body position.**

Ball-you-man: These are the three most important factors in defensive basketball—(1) the ball; (2) you, the defensive player; (3) the man you are guarding. Any time your man does not have the ball, you must be between your man and the ball. But any time we have a ball-man-you alignment, the defensive man is neither in position to help nor to prevent his man from getting the basketball.

> **NOTE: There are several drills that we can use to teach this ball-you-man defensive position. Some will be covered later in this article.**

Flat-triangle concept: Each one of our men is part of a triangle the points of which are his man, the ball, and himself. The base of the triangle is a line drawn from his man to the ball. The defensive man forms the apex.

There are essentially three rules to follow in establishing the triangle:

1. Never be more than one step off the base of the triangle, which we call the line of the ball.

2. The ball-side defender must be close enough to the ball to stop penetration by use of the dribble or the pass if he is in the back line.

3. The further the ball is from your man, the further you can be from the man.

> **NOTE: The ball-you-man and flat-triangle concept terms used by Coach Knight have made it much easier for our defensive players to see their relationship to their teammates, as well as their responsibility in team defense.**

Help and recover: This term refers to the player getting into position to help stop penetration of the ball and then recovering to his own man. A defensive player who has helped stop penetration but does not recover in time to prevent his man from scoring is not doing his job.

In playing team defense, we usually find ourselves in positions that require player-to-player communication or an understanding of rules that are to be followed as a defensive situation presents itself.

> **EXAMPLE: For example, when the guards cross, we must have a rule so that our defensive men know whether they are to slide through or to fight over the top. In our defensive preparation, when we are inside of 20 feet, we like our defensive players to fight over the top. If we can fight over the top and stay in position to prevent the outside shot, we feel we are playing sound defense inside of 20 feet.**

If the offensive player is outside the 20-foot range or the high-percentage scoring area, we allow our players to slide through. In sliding through, they will find themselves one man removed from the ball. We never want to be two men removed from the ball.

Drill Program

These terms are all basic in teaching good team defense. We found we took it for granted that our players actually understood what each of these terms meant in playing defense. But since we explained all these terms in a defensive handbook, which is distributed to all players, our defensive game has improved considerably.

DRILLS: With each of these terms, drills are used to teach—the flat-triangle concept; the ball-you-man relationship; sliding through; fighting over the top; being one man removed, but never two men removed from the ball.

In early-season individual defensive work, we spend a considerable amount of time on stance, making the drop step, closing out on the basketball, retreating and defensive footwork. As we progress into team defensive play, the situations of helping, two-man and three-man defensive basketball become a daily practice routine.

The following drills are a few used in teaching individual and team defense:

Slide through: As shown in Diagram 1, this starts with a dribble to

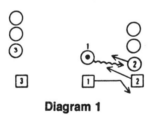

Diagram 1

either side with   1   in a good defensive shuffle with his head on the ball. As he approaches his teammate who is talking to him and yelling "let me through,"   1   gives ground and lets   2   slide through.

NOTE: The same is repeated as   2   approaches   3   with   3   talking and letting his teammate know his position. The drill is run from sideline to sideline with the dribbler going to the end of the line and a new dribbler taking his place on each exchange.

Zig-zag: Using half the floor from the lane line to the sideline, the

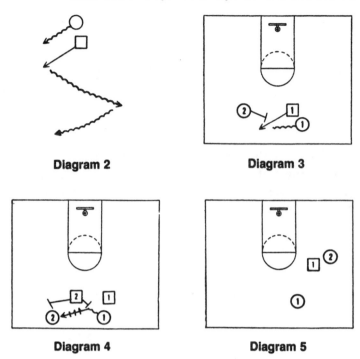

Diagram 2   **Diagram 3**

Diagram 4   **Diagram 5**

defensive player moves with his hands behind his back concentrating on footwork with his "head on the ball" and making the drop step when the change of direction occurs (Diagram 2).

Fighting over the top: In this drill (Diagram 3),   2   sets a front screen and   1   tries to drive   1   into the screen or reverse direction to keep   1   honest.   1   must fight over the screen to prevent   1   from getting a shot or going all the way to the goal.

Help and recover: In this guard-to-guard situation (Diagram 4),   1   forces   1   to the middle where his penetration is stopped by   2   2   then must recover to   2   to stop shot or prevent drive.

> **NOTE: At first, limit offense to shot only, then add drive and cut by second offensive player. The same situation can be set up involving guard and forward.**

Ball-you-man and guard-to-forward pass: This is a 1-on-1 situation after the first pass if   1   does not succeed in preventing the pass (Diagram 5). We limit the area of the offensive man early in the season emphasizing the position of the defensive man.

> **NOTE: If   2   does make the reverse cut, we want   1   to "open up" by pivoting on his back foot, staying in visual**

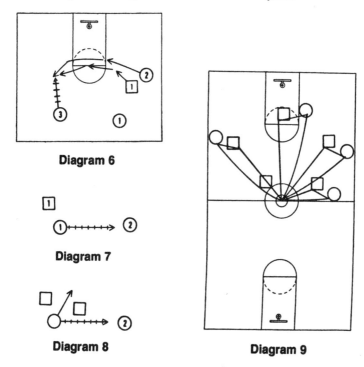

Diagram 6

Diagram 7

Diagram 8

Diagram 9

contact with the ball at all times. A continuation of this drill would be for   2   to continue across the lane with   1   fronting him all the way and pressuring the guard. Diagram 6 shows the forward pass on the opposite side of the floor.

Ball-you-man: In this defensive guard-to-guard situation,   1   passes to   2   . On the pass   1   establishes his ball-you-man relationship by moving toward the ball. See Diagram 7.

NOTE: In establishing this position, we are forcing the offensive man to go behind. See Diagram 8.

Flat triangle: In this drill (Diagram 9) we pass the basketball to different positions on the floor and move every player so he can determine his position in relation to his teammates.

Part IV

Organization & Practice

1

An Individual Analysis Sheet for High School Basketball

by Herb Livsey

Head Basketball Coach
Orange Coast Junior College
Costa Mesa, California

Herb Livsey coached high school basketball from 1958 to 1969 in Florida, Nevada, and northern and southern California. He was twice named Coach-of-the-Year in the Pioneer League in northern California, and gained his 100th career win when coaching at Costa Mesa High School in southern California. He is presently at Orange Coast College where his teams have finished in the first division of the tough South Coast Conference three of the past four years.

Basketball coaches at all levels critically evaluate their players' skills and performances throughout the year. We have tried to supplement such critical evaluation of each player with a rating sheet (Chart I). This we feel enables the player to see a more tangible analysis of his strengths and weaknesses.

NOTE: The idea for such an evaluation of young players was borrowed from Bob Cousy, head coach at Boston College, when this writer was employed as a counselor at Camp Graylag, Bob's basketball camp for boys in Pittsfield, New Hampshire.

BASKETBALL INDIVIDUAL RATING SHEET Player				COSTA MESA HIGH SCHOOL 196_ — 196_
Phase of Game	**Excellent** **Good**	**Fair**	**Weak**	**Comments**
Attitude				
Aggressiveness				
Stamina				
Concentration in Learning				
Execution of Drills				
Basketball Sense				
Mental Alertness in game				
Fundamentals				
Speed or Quickness				
Defensive Ability: On Ball				
Away from Ball				
Rebounding: Defensive				
Rebounding: Offensive				
Offensive Ability: Passing				
Dribbling				
Pass receiving				
Cutting				
Moving without ball				
Screening				
Feinting & Drive				
Lay-ups				
Foul shooting				
Jump shooting				
Outside shooting				
Pivot shots				
Corner shots				
Offensive Summary:				

Chart I

The rating sheet has since been revised several times to its present form, and has been used successfully in the total high school program at Costa Mesa High School in southern California (varsity, junior varsity, sophomore, and frosh teams) and at the Snow Valley Basketball School during August of each year in the San Bernardino Mountains in California.

Evaluation: At Costa Mesa High School we have used the evaluation both at mid-year and at the end of the season. At mid-season we have an individual conference with each player concerning his present progress; at the close of the season we expect a boy to begin to concentrate on those areas where he has been rated below "good."

DRILLS: The individual fundamental drills we have employed throughout the playing season will help him in his concentration.

Each sheet is completed in duplicate and a file kept on each returning player for the scrutiny of the coach the following year. Senior players who are going on to college have a complete file for interested college recruiters. Such evaluation also requires each coach to concentrate on the individual and team abilities of each of his players.

Wide acceptance: At the Snow Valley Basketball School we have had many high school and junior high school players from the western United States who have made good use of their rating sheets. Letters are received often which relate experiences in which the boys have improved from concentrating hard on areas where the staff has rated them below acceptable ability.

COMMENTS: The comments are highly important for the completeness of the analysis. The coach must discuss fully all areas which he feels the boy must practice to improve. The player must understand what is being required of him. The coach and player usually follow up a discussion of the rating sheet with some extra work on the court.

2

Practice Organization:
Key to Success

by Royce Youree

Head Basketball Coach
East High School
Phoenix, Arizona

Coach Youree's teams at East High School have an eight-year varsity record of 123 wins against 66 losses. This includes three league championships, three Christmas Holiday tournament championships, and two state AAA championships. Coach Youree holds two "Coach-of-the-Year" awards. His overall varsity record is 160-75.

I don't believe anyone will argue the fact that within all of us lies the desire to be successful. This is especially true in the area of athletics, which indeed has become more and more competitive each year. Bearing this in mind and relating it to coaching basketball, I'm sure that all of us want to do everything in our power to be winners. I firmly believe that practice organization can be a major key to reaching that goal.

NOTE: This article shows how we organize our practices here at East High School. It's not meant to imply that ours is the best or only way. It has simply proven successful for us and perhaps will prove profitable to your program in some way.

Practice Sheet

I devised a basketball practice sheet when I came to East High School seven years ago. The original concept was to list all of the individual, group, and team drills that would make up our seasonal master practice plan. I abbreviated the major headings and listed the appropriate drills under each one, as shown in Chart I.

CHART I

Varsity Coach–Royce R. Youree | Frosh Coach (Purple) Hector Bejarano
J. V. Coach–Darryl D. Franz | Frosh Coach (Scarlett) Ken Golash

EAST HIGH SCHOOL BASKETBALL PRACTICE SHEET

Date_____ Team_____ Coach_____

Time_____ Schedule_____ Time_____ Schedule_____

PA– PASSING
1 Face Drill
2 Running Face Drill
3 4-Square Drill
4 3-man fig. 8–½ Crt. & Full
5 5-man fig. 8–full Crt.
6 2-Ball Peripheral

S – SHOOTING & PASSING
1 Dribble Jumps
2 Pass, Return Pass
3 Challenge Dribble Jps.
4 "Zig Zag" Drill
5 Fast-break Jumps
6 "Golf" Drills
7 Free Throws
8 Fundamentals
9 5-man Jump or Drive

LA – LAY-UPS & PASSING
1 Dribble
2 Pass, Return Pass
3 Fast Break
4 2-on-1, 3-on-2
5 "Challenge" Dribble
6 "Zig Zag" Drill

PI – PIVOTING (STOPPING)
1 Manipulation
2 Reverse-Pivot Ball

DR – DRIBBLING
1 "Line" Drill
2 "Circle" Drill
3 "Weave" Drill with Baseball Pass
4 Tag
5 Blinders

OB – OUT-OF-BOUNDS PLAYS (MAN & ZONE)
1 Underneath Basket
2 Sidelines
3 Last Sec. Shot

REB – REBOUNDING
1 3-vs.-3 (2 outlet man)
2 Strong side (2 on 2)
3 Weak side (2 on 2)
4 2-on-1
5 2nd effort
6 1-on-1, 2-on-2
7 Reaction

FB – FAST BREAK
1 3-man Skeleton
2 5-man Skeleton
3 3 Off. Rebounders, Spoiler & 2 Def. Men
4 From Free Throw
5 From Jump Ball
6 5 on 5

M.OFF – MAN OFFENSE
1 2-3 Regular
2 Strong Post
3 Passing Game
4 Delay Game
5 1-3-1 Movement
6 Last Sec. Shot
7 2-min. Offense

Z.OFF–ZONE OFFENSE
1 1-3-1 Movement
2 Round Off
3 2-Guard Front
4 Delay Game
5 Last Sec. Shot

JB – JUMP BALLS
1 Offensive
2 Defensive
3 Neutral

COND. – CONDITIONING
1 3-on-2–2-on-1 continuation
2 Middle Line
3 F B Weave (3 men)
4 Blitz

PR – PRESSES (OFF. & DEF.)
1 Man (Full Court)
2 Man (3/4 Crt. & ½ Crt.)
3 UCLA
4 3-2 (½ Crt.)
5 1-3-1 Zone (3/4 & ½ Crt.)
6 2-2-1 Zone (3/4 Crt.)
7 2-1-2 Zone (3/4 Crt.)

OFF-DEF – OFFENSIVE-DEFENSIVE DRILLS
1 1-on-1 (Drives Outside & Inside) Passive & Active
2 1-on-1 (Full & ½ Crt.)
3 2-on-2
4 3-on-3 (Full & ½ Crt.)
5 2-on-1
6 3-on-2
7 3-on-3 inside game with passer

DEF – DEFENSIVE DRILLS
1 "Face" Drill
2 2-Guard Front Drill
3 2-Guard & Post Drill
4 1-Guard & Forward Drill
5 2-Guard & 1-Forward Drill
6 2-Guard & 2-Forward (Cutting-off Passing Lanes Drill–Skeleton & Live)
7 "Post" Drill
8 Guarding Man Without Ball Drill
9 Two Forwards & Post Drill
10 5-man Skeleton Def. Drill
11 1-Guard Offense & Post Drill

Z.OFF-DEF – ZONE OFF. & DEF.
1 2-1-2
2 1-2-2
3 1-3-1
4 Box and Chaser, Triangle and Chaser
5 Match-up

**EXAMPLE: Time 3:15; REB 3—which is weakside re-
bounding 2-on-2. One of the responsibilities of our mana-
gers is to handle the practice sheet and make sure that we
stay on schedule.**

Checklist

Another concept of immense importance is that the practice sheet can
and should be used as a checklist. This eliminates any needless guesswork
as to what you have or have not covered. You can circle the items you
wish to cover the next day while you are making out the daily practice
plan—and therefore not be subject to forgetfulness.

You can also, on a separate practice sheet, mark down the number of
times you have done each drill and how much time you have spent on
each. At the end of the year, you will know exactly how much time was
spent on each drill and how much time on offense and defense. This way
you are leaving nothing to chance.

Coaching Unity

The unity of our coaching staff has definitely been helped by this
organization plan. We have two frosh teams in addition to our junior
varsity and varsity teams—and our entire staff uses the same practice
plan.

It has helped to make sure that we are all doing the same drills with
proper emphasis on each, and to have the same basketball philosophy.
Unity is just as important to the coaching staff as it is to the team, and I
know this practice sheet has helped us to "think-alike" which is a must.

Update Practice Sheet

It should be pointed out here that we have pre-season staff meetings to
update our practice sheet as needed. Also, at these meetings we make
certain that all coaches are knowledgeable concerning everything that is
on the practice sheet.

**NOTE: During this time, coaching ideas and techniques
are implanted in each coach's mind. We also conduct several staff meetings each week during the season to insure
that everything is running smoothly.**

Summary

In summary, this practice sheet has definitely helped to make us better organized in our practice procedures. We use the sheet as a daily practice plan and checklist and for uniting our coaching staff with the same coaching philosophy.

> **NOTE: While many factors enter into the success of a basketball program, we're convinced that good organization is a major key to that success—and in this respect our practice sheet has proven profitable for us.**

3

Theories of Practice Organization

by John Rendek

Assistant Basketball Coach
University of Tulsa
Tulsa, Oklahoma

*John Rendek began coaching high school basketball in
1956. At Crofton High School (Crofton, Kentucky) he compiled a three-year record of 70-17 which included two district
titles; at Christian County High School (Hopkinsville, Kentucky) his record was 91-21 with three district titles and one
regional title; at Male High School (Louisville, Kentucky) he
posted a 91-19 record with four district titles and one regional.*

The importance of pre-planned and organized practice sessions can not
be overemphasized. The successful coach must be able to account for his
practice time and know what portion of that time he is giving to offense,
defense, verbal instruction, and other phases of the game.

**PLAN: The structure of the plan is very insignificant; the
thing of importance is that you have one. True, these plans
might be altered several times before completion—but the
basic structural idea will remain.**

In this article we'll cover some of our theories on basketball practice organization and the selection of drills. Some of these ideas and theories are original and others were secured through observation, clinics, literature and informal discussions. They have served as our guidelines—and whatever success we have enjoyed, we must give partial credit to them.

Practice Planning

There are several factors that the coach should consider in planning for his pre-season practice schedule—and such planning should be done in the summer months or early fall.

Team play: How do you plan to have your team play? Are you going to put emphasis on the running game or are you planning to exercise the control game? A survey of returning personnel will help you to decide. If you have experienced boys returning, with good board control, you might favor the running game. On the other hand, if you're hit heavy by graduation, you might be nursing ball-control ideas. Whatever your choice, drills must be employed to match your style of play.

Plan strategy: How do you expect to carry out your plan? Some coaches prefer the scrimmage situation as a means of instruction, conditioning, and player selection. Others favor the use of fundamental drills working toward the perfection of the individual. The important thing here is to determine your plan and follow it.

COACHING AID: Players learn better if they have an understanding of the relationship of one phase of the pattern of play to another. We use our first practice session as an orientation day. Besides explaining basic procedures, we tell our candidates what offensive and defensive structures we plan to use.

Drill philosophy: In selecting drills, emphasis should be placed not only on the drill's suitability in furthering the total offensive or defensive plan, but also in perfecting individual techniques. For example, in teaching our defensive structure to our squad, we would first stress sound individual defensive fundamentals—such as stance, lateral movement, backward movement, etc.

NOTE: This would be accomplished through the use of one-man and group drills. We would then progress to two-and three-man drills before going to half-court and full-court team work.

We drill until perfection is attained—and here are some facts in this respect. Fifty percent of what is learned is forgotten within 24 hours. Within two weeks, no more than ten percent is retained. So we always repeat without fail the same drills the day following their introduction. We feel that learning is better retained when drills are practiced in several short periods—rather than in a few long periods.

Mental staleness: A point is reached where improvement slows down—so the coach should be alert for mental staleness about the middle of the season. We always look for irritability among players as a sign of mental staleness and remedy the situation by giving time off from practice.

> **TIP: Coaches must understand that boys reach a plateau where they must have time to digest the information they have been fed thus far. Any new material at this point could have a bad effect on the entire squad.**

Teaching devices: The use of various teaching devices will enhance learning. We use game films, films on fundamental execution, etc., as teaching aids. We also distribute mimeographed materials to the players—on offensive and defensive systems and their execution. The bulletin board, of course, is widely used in this respect.

Practice sessions: Our practice sessions vary in length from two and a half hours in the pre-season sessions—to 50 minutes when approaching tournament time. How much time you allot the different phases of the game will be dictated by the coach's philosophy. The major portion of our practice time has always been given to team and individual defense. We feel that defense is the rallying point of our entire program—that it is the ultimate weapon of pressure basketball and the very backbone of our offensive attack.

> **NOTE: Here again, this is my theory—so consequently it is reflected in our practice plan.**

Drill Program

Our offensive and defensive drills are usually two-, three- and four-man breakdown maneuvers of our total team structure. Naturally, the drills used during the pre-season period lean heavily toward conditioning—these become less strenuous when the season begins.

> **NOTE: Drills which emphasize the execution of fundamentals are used all year long. These are short and snappy and competitive whenever possible.**

All-Purpose drill: Every coach has his favorite drill—ours is called the "all-purpose" drill. We got the idea from Ed Jucker's "11-man" drill —and made some modifications to include our entire squad. The drill is most complete and comes closer to creating a game situation on a practice court than any drill I know.

NOTE: It creates the three-on-two situation, provides the transition from defense to offense, teaches rebounding, ball release and lane filling—all necessary ingredients of a sound running game. We use this drill all season long.

As shown in Diagram 1, the coach puts the ball upon the boards. Let's assume that X1 rebounds it. As he does, players in front of mid-court

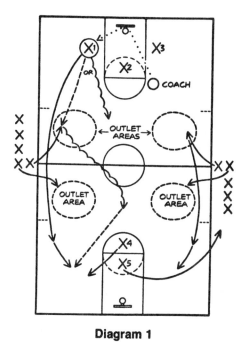

Diagram 1

lines fill the outlet areas. X1 has two options—he could release the ball to the player in the outlet area on his side, or he could "kick" out with it on the dribble.

Let's further assume that he releases to the outlet—outlet man dribbles to middle lane—weakside outlet man floods outside lane on his side—and the rebounder fills the wide lane on his side. These three people attack X4 and X5, the two defenders.

NOTE: This 3-2 situation will continue until the offense scores, or the defense rebounds. If a goal is made, either

X4 or X5 will grab the ball and the situation reverses toward the other end. If, for instance X4 rebounds—then X5
will go in one of the side lanes, and two of the three men
who were on offense will remain on defense.

Practice Schedule

Chart I is a sample copy of our pre-season practice schedule at Male
High School. It was designed so that practice for the coming season
would include pressing tactics, team defense, fast break, free lance and
screen offense. The "thought gem" changes daily.

PRE-SEASON PRACTICE SCHEDULE

Male High School

THOUGHT GEM:	Coming together is a begin-ning, keeping together is success.
2:15–2:20	Warm-up—finger flexing, ball ro-tation, bench jumping.
2:20–2:25	Agility drills.
2:25–2:40	Spot shooting.
2:40–2:50	Group drills—touch rim, touch board, tipping, rotating.
2:50–3:00	Basket play—guard and forward fakes, pivot maneuvers.
3:00–3:05	Dribbling drills—half-court and full-court.
3:05–3:15	Free-throws and running.
3:15–3:25	Passing drills—on the spot, bull in the ring, fire ball.
3:25–3:40	Two-man automatics—hand back and roll, hand back and return pass, hand back and hesitate, check-off, pick and roll, pass and cut behind, take around.
3:40–3:55	All-purpose drill (Diagram 1).
3:55–4:00	Free-throws and running.
4:00–4:30	Defensive drills—full-court cutoff, switching, going through, going over the top, guarding base line, defensing shuffle.
4:30–4:35	Pressure free-throws.
4:35–4:45	Close outs—figure eight, rotating eight break.

Chart I

4

A Basic Daily Practice Plan

by Dean Nicholson

Head Basketball Coach
Central Washington State College
Ellensburg, Washington

As head basketball coach at Central Washington State, Dean Nicholson has guided his squads to four consecutive NAIA district championships with records of 20-6, 21-8, 27-4, and 22-8. His 1967 squad took third place in the NAIA nationals and the 1968 squad won the quarter-final round. In 1969, his team took third place in the NAIA nationals and second place in 1970. Coach Nicholson was NAIA "Coach-of-the-Year" in 1970. His overall record is 206-64.

Our basic practice plan is based on a two-hour and 15-minute practice. Of course, all practices are adjusted according to the time of the season, physical and psychological state of the team, nearness of games, strength of opponent, etc.

NOTE: However, we do feel that having a basic daily plan from which to function is very advantageous. All daily practice plans are kept in a notebook, and practice statistics recorded.

The daily practice plan is detailed as follows:

1. Open unit: We spend 10 to 15 minutes on a warm-up. The squad is divided into three groups, and three to five minutes are spent at each of three stations—(a) rope skipping; (b) calisthenics; (c) split-vision passing drill (two balls with a group of four).

TIP: We found that relying upon the players to do the above on their own during a free-shooting period did not give us the desired results—thus, the reason for the opening unit.

2. Free shooting (20 minutes): Here we stress concentration, shooting the shots that will be used in a game, and proper footwork execution. It is easy to fall into a rut and actually practice bad habits daily during this phase of the workout—thus, we stress doing it the right way.

NOTE: We want game-situation practice, such as shooting after a drive or pass reception at game speed. Also, we want our post man working with an outside feeder.

3. Lay-in drills (10 minutes): We shoot four types of driving shots—(a) normal lay-in from the side; (b) drive under and reverse lay-in; (c) the shovel or gliding type of underhand shot; (d) cross-over—driving through the key and shooting a semi-hook off the corner of the board (Diagram 1).

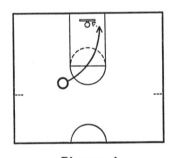

Diagram 1

TIP: We stress a "limp" shooting wrist and two-handed control of the ball in our driving shots.

4. Fast break unit (10 minutes): We work on one or two of the following (a) 2-on-1 or 3-on-2; (b) rebound and outlet drill; (c) 5-on-0 break; (d) 5-on-2 or 5-on-3; (e) fast-break drill (Diagram 2).

EXECUTION: Our fast break drill is continuous 4-on-2. Twelve players (three groups of four) are needed to run it. Example: four whites break against two red defenders with

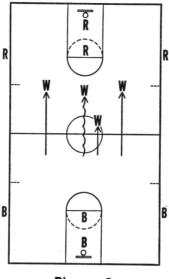

Diagram 2

two other reds waiting at outlet spots. **When reds gain possession (steal, rebound or score), they react and break with three lanes and a trailer against two blue defenders with two more blues waiting in the wings. If a man plays defense at one end, he will be an outlet at the other end.**

5. 1-on-1 unit (10 minutes): (a) defense a drive with hands clasped behind the back; (b) defense a weakside offensive man; (c) live 1-on-1 versus the ball; (d) press the dribbler on half-court width.

NOTE: The above five workouts can be accomplished in approximately one hour.

6. Pivot, dribble, tip unit (5 minutes): (a) three-man footwork drill; (b) free-lance dribbling (two 30-second bursts); (c) one minute of tipping.

7. Free throwing (5 minutes): We throw two at a time and stress getting a good look at the basket before release from a chin high position—with no foot movement during the shot.

8. Group work (10 minutes): We work here (2-on-2; 3-on-3; 4-on-4) on specific parts of our offensive motion or against different defensive situations.

9. Mass defense (3 minutes): Players assume defensive stance and follow a ''leader.'' We use half of the team at each end of the floor, employing three 30-second bursts at each end.

10. Teamwork (15 to 20 minutes): This is a controlled scrimmage with the top unit (seven or eight players) on defense. We fast break off any steal or rebound, but return to defense as soon as the break is over.

> **NOTE: If press work is desired, the offense may full-court press after every score, then return to offense again after press situation is completed.**

11. Offensive timing (5 minutes): Here we work 5-on-0.

12. Teamwork (15 minutes): Again, this is a controlled scrimmage——same as previous teamwork with top unit on offense.

13. Free throwing (2 minutes): Same as previous free throwing.

14. Scrimmage (10 to 30 minutes): We scrimmage under game conditions. If more than a 10-minute scrimmage is desired, other units of work will be shortened or eliminated.

15. Run lines (3 minutes): Here we do one, two or three sets. End line to foul line and return, to midline and return, far foul line and return, then opposite end line and return.

Conditioning Program

We recommend a four-week preseason conditioning program involving a minimum of 30 minutes per day. This includes:

Rope skip: We do this 5 minutes daily—rest as often as necessary the first two weeks, but keep it humming.

Calisthenics: These include fingertip push-ups, bent leg sit-ups, groin stretcher, and saddle jumps—5 minutes daily.

Walk: Walk on the inside and outside of feet for a minute each way——daily.

Catch: Play catch with heavyweight basketballs or medicine balls—5 minutes daily.

Isometrics: We do basic isometrics.

Running: We run one mile per day the first two weeks, then other distances—440 and 880.

> **NOTE: Each boy is timed early and at the end of the program for the mile, for evaluation of individual improvement.**

Sprints: We run ten 30-yard sprints at 4-second intervals. The goal is to maintain a "best" time level throughout the ten sprints. Two times are necessary, one at each end of the 30-yard distance. Each boy sprints the 30 yards one way, then returns in the opposite direction after a 4-second rest.

5

Successful Practices—
Successful Seasons

by Stan DuFrane

Head Basketball Coach
Craig High School
Janesville, Wisconsin

Stan DuFrane has been coaching high school and college basketball for 17 years and has an overall record of 247-138. The last nine years he has been head coach at Craig High School. During fourteen years of high school coaching, Coach DuFrane has had many All-Conference players plus All-American Tim Patrick who is a Junior at the University of Wisconsin; Geoff Kraus who is a Freshman at Northern Illinois; Bob Schmidt who graduated from Georgia Tech; and All-State Lyle Papenfuss who played at Winona State College, Minnesota. His teams have been conference champions the last two of three years.

I firmly believe that a well-planned practice is a successful practice, and that successful practices mean successful seasons. Here's the way we go about planning and conducting our practice sessions at Craig High School.

Early Planning

Early in September we begin preparing for our basketball season. From our knowledge of returning players we complete our basic plan for offensive and defensive formations and practices.

NOTE: Last season we had one outstanding player (All-American Tim Patrick) to start the season and several good players. Next season we know that we will have three very good big men and must develop some good guards.

Keeping these points in mind, we formulate all offensive and defensive formations. Because we will be playing three big boys and every team in our conference will be trying to neutralize our height advantage with a full-court press, it will be necessary for our team to work daily against pressing defenses. Knowing this, our boys will be ready for plenty of full-court, three-on-three, double-teaming practice sessions.

Daily Practices

After individual shooting, our daily formal practices usually begin with either the running of ten laps or our defensive stance drill in which we have the players move right, left, forward, or backward with emphasis on the sliding of the feet, feinting, changing of pace, changing of direction, pivoting, and body position.

NOTE: The length of time varies from day to day, from three minutes normally to fifteen minutes if necessary.

Lay-up drills are used to encourage accuracy and to promote jumping and dunking, which all add to our team spirit. The figure 8 drill is run from sideline to sideline with emphasis on full-court lay-ups and passing. I believe that passing is one of the most important fundamentals of basketball. Accurate passes often contribute to scoring; inaccurate passes usually lead to missed baskets. Accurate passing increases shooting percentages.

Fast Break 3-on-2; 2-on-1 drill: This drill (Diagram 1) begins with the outlet pass from the middle man, O1 dribbling after the ball gets to half-court. The two defensive men, D1 and D2, play tandem defense. We look for the short jumper.

NOTE: After the shot, O1 plays defense and D1 and D2 advance the ball up court without dribbling (Diagram 2). Here we look for the lay-up.

Trap drill: We developed the trap drill (Diagram 3) when the double-teaming defenses became so prominent. Two defensive players, D1 and

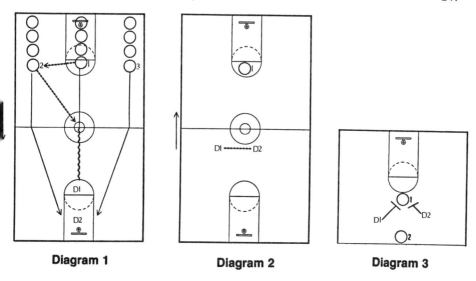

| Diagram 1 | Diagram 2 | Diagram 3 |

D2, start between two offensive players, O1 and O2, who are spaced about 5 to 7 yards apart.

> **NOTE: D1 and D2 attack the ball and trap O1. O1 must pass the ball to O2. After the offensive players have each been trapped two or three times the players change positions—the two defensive players becoming the offensive players.**

The trap drill has helped our teams considerably to withstand pressure. It proves to the players that they can get out of a double-team easily without panicking.

> **NOTE: During each practice we spend a few minutes working on tip-off plays and jump-ball situations. In the last few years our players have controlled 75½ of jump balls. All jump-ball situations are covered during these drill periods.**

Free-throw rebound drill: This drill is used to control rebounds from missed free throws. When we use this drill the coach shoots the ball and misses—and all players go for the rebound.

> **NOTE: D1 and D2 screen out under the basket; D5 screens out the shooter; D4 either moves into the lane or behind D1; D3 either plays out to the side or on the lane (Diagrams 4 and 5).**

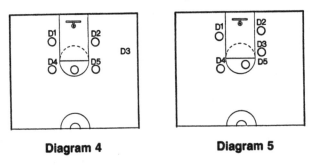

Diagram 4   **Diagram 5**

No player is allowed to dribble an offensive rebound; he may pass or shoot. The first team to control five offensive rebounds or to score six points is the winner. The losing team then runs the lines.

Eight years ago our team lost three games in a row because our players did a poor job of screening out on missed free throws. This drill is now a part of our daily routine and the results in games are much more satisfactory.

When we use the rebound drill we emphasize offensive rebounding as well as scoring. If the offensive team scores or controls the offensive rebound, it has the ball again for another attempt. If it loses the ball, the defensive team becomes the offensive team.

> **NOTE: We play for ten points, one point for each offensive board and one point for each basket. Again the losers run the lines. By keeping an offensive rebound count and basket score we bring a little fun into practice and keep interest high.**

Other Practice Techniques

Our practices include one-on-one games to ten baskets, with the loser running the lines. Free-throw games of ten shots, two at a time, are shot against the same opponent with the loser again running the lines. These back-to-back games put some pressure on the boys and also force them to shoot, even when tired.

Our teams use the scoreboard and clock in practice two or three times a week for running game situations that include jump balls, offensive plays, defensive formation, free-throws, out-of-bounds plays, stalling tactics, and last-minute situations. During the last several years our teams have played many close games. The use of the scoreboard and the clock gives us practice in using time to our advantage.

100% drill: Most of our practices end with the 100% drill. The boys line up in three lines—figure 8 up the court; attempt the basket; return. If all three complete the drill perfectly they are released from the drill. These players then may cheer or chide the other players until all complete the drill without error. You can tell by how much noise they make at this point just how much "vinegar" they have left.

Swing-Man Theory

While much has been written about fundamentals, team defense and team offense, very little has been written concerning substitution during a game. Our practices are planned with the idea of a starting seven. We use three guards and four pivot men.

NOTE: One guard and one pivot man are the "swing men" for those positions. The inside swing man must know all three inside positions with all options. The outside swing man must know the two guard positions with all the options. For example, swing man O6 takes over O5's position. When O5 re-enters the game for O3, O5 returns to his own position and O6 takes over O3's corner position (see Diagrams 6 and 7).

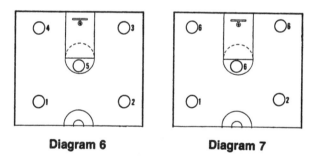

Diagram 6   **Diagram 7**

With this system we know who our number 1 substitute will be for the under positions and the outside positions. We are already aware of his strong points and his weak points and we know where he can contribute the most to the team.

The use of the swing man has psychologically aided our team when a player has become ill right before game time. Before we started using the swing-man system, we often felt that a lack, or excess, of substitutions cost us games because of fatigue or lack of continuity. The swing-man system has helped players develop confidence in their teammates.

Award System

In planning our practices each week we take into consideration the results of the "Cougar Award" chart (Cougars is our nickname). The Cougar Award for the week is given to the player who accumulated in the last game the most award points in the following categories:

1) Field goal percentage.
2) Free-throw percentage.
3) Rebounds.
4) Fewest Errors.
5) Gains.
6) Assists.
7) Tie-ups.

Award points are earned on a ten-point basis. For example, the player with the best field-goal percentage in the last game gets ten points; the player with the next best field-goal percentage in the last game gets nine points; and so on down the line in each of the categories.

The player who earned the most award points in the game gets the Cougar Award for that week. By studying the results of these charts, we can determine the areas in which we need the most work and the players who need the most help. We then plan our practice sessions accordingly.

6

Prepractice Preparation

by John Nese

Head Basketball Coach
Central Catholic High School
Steubenville, Ohio

John Nese has been coaching high school basketball for 13 years, the last ten at Central Catholic. The last three years his teams have won 59 games, losing only 11. His teams were beaten by the eventual state champs the last two years in the regionals. Coach Nese is presently retired from coaching and teaches at Central Catholic.

In my 11 years of coaching, I have always wanted to have some form of standardized activity for the first 20 to 30 minutes of practice that would cover in a short period of time important fundamentals of basketball.

After talking with other coaches, reading articles on the subject, and discussing it with our players, we have devised such an activity—an approximate 25-minute routine to be used at the beginning of each of our practices.

Station Drills

Our practice time is limited because we don't have our own gym, so it is important that we make the most of our time. Each day the players are required to loosen up by taking two laps and doing a short series of ankle exercises.

After five minutes of free shooting, we begin our practice by moving into our station drills (Figure 1). Each player has a partner whom he stays with for two days.

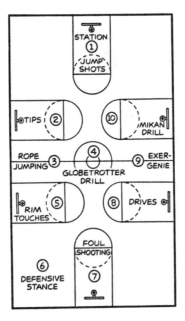

Diagram 1

NOTE: We have approximately 20 boys involved in these drills. They are at each station two minutes and on the whistle they have ten seconds to move to the next station.

Station 1.   JUMP SHOOTING—shoot jump shot from 15 feet and in. Follow shot and try to rebound before it hits the ground. Make lay-up and dribble out and repeat.

Station 2.   CONSECUTIVE TIPS—tip ball with right hand at least even with the rim. Do the same with left hand. Guards 15, Big Men 20.

Station 3.   ROPE JUMPING—Work on different routines to help improve coordination.

Station 4.   GLOBETROTTER DRILL—keep the ball moving rapidly behind the back and through the legs for one minute. Also for one minute practice dribble routine using cross-over, behind back, through-the-legs, etc.

Station 5.   RIM TOUCHES—we also use bottom of board or net depending on size of player. Goal is ten straight touches. At times we make the player jump continuously for one minute.

Station 6.   DEFENSIVE STANCE—assume good defensive position, one foot slightly forward, weight on balls of feet, slightly crouched with palms up. Move in a rectangular motion.

Station 7.   FOUL SHOOTING—we normally shoot five foul shots, but at times we use the one-and-one, and if both are made, player can shoot three more.

Station 8.   DRIVES—start at foul line; one day we go right, next day left. We use different moves, e.g. fake left, go right; fake right, go left.

Station 9.   EXER-GENIE—use Big 4 exercises. Two repitions.

Station 10.   MIKAN DRILL—start under basket. Shoot right-hand lay-up or semi-hook, rebound and in a continuous motion shoot left-hand lay-up; repeat. Goal is ten straight.

NOTE: While these drills are going on my assistant coaches are in different areas watching, suggesting, correcting and helping the boys carry out these drills.

Conclusion

Many of the drills mentioned are familiar ones and are probably used by most coaches at one time or another during their practice sessions.

The particular 10 that we use are ones we like best. However, substitutions can be made to an individual coach's liking and stations can be added or deleted depending on time, available space, and facilities.

We have been using the station setup the past three years and have found it to be very advantageous to our program. I highly recommend it as a practice tool to be used at all levels of competition.

Part V

Philosophy

1

Principles of Sound Basketball Coaching

by Jack Jaquet

Former Head Basketball Coach
York College of Pennsylvania
York, Pennsylvania

Jack Jaquet has been coaching high school and college basketball for some 19 years, and has never had a losing season. During that time he has had his share of league and district titles. Since 1960, Coach Jaquet has been head basketball coach at York Junior College (now a 4-year college known as York College of Pennsylvania). His overall mark is an impressive 258-128. He is now retired from coaching, and is chairman of the physical education and athletics department at York College.

In some 19 years of coaching high school and college basketball I've been lucky enough never to have suffered through a losing season—and I like to think that my own efforts helped the players achieve this record.

NO MAGIC FORMULA: However, my emphasis is on the word "efforts." I don't claim to have brilliant ideas that would be a revelation to other coaches. In short, I will not describe or diagram a "magic formula."

Instead, I'd like to offer some advice to young coaches. The following outline is a set of principles that have served me well. In addition, these ideas have been passed on to a good many young coaches who received undergraduate training from me; they tell me such thinking proved to be a good foundation on which to build.

System of play: Don't copy another coach's system just because he's having a great year or two. Choose a style of play that you yourself know best. It may be a system you were taught as a player or in a college coaching class. Study your system so that you know its limitations as well as its strengths.

> **NOTE: Watch others. There are no copyrights in basketball; you can take home anything you see—don't overdo it, though. If you really know your own system, you can adapt new ideas to it. Rather than using a mass of new techniques, take only the best.**

> **FOR INSTANCE: Naturally, there are formations and patterns that you'll be sold on. I'm convinced that the 2-1-2 single post offensive alignment, with only minor variations in positioning the post man, is the one single starting formation I seek from which my teams will attack today's great variety of defenses.**

My personal system for sound balance is to pattern team floor circulation so that some combination of three team members is always concerned with getting offensive board position; one man is in an intermediate position to either supplement an offensive move or to fall back quickly; the fifth man is strictly concerned with providing his front-court teammates assurance that they can always get the ball back out to start over or to become an immediate defensive safety if we lose the ball.

Keep it simple: Two or three simple continuing patterns are an adequate set offense—if your players fully understand all their options and possibilities. Coaching is teaching. Players aren't chessmen a coach can move about. They must know the possibilities of their patterns. They must both know situations and be able to create the situation they want.

> **NOTE: Use a chalkboard a lot. Have one at the edge of your practice floor. Keep it simple but thorough. Players must act with complete awareness of the thinking underlying their movement. You will use some type of signals and they too should be kept simple. I happen to prefer ball-handling signals.**

Man-to-man defense: Teach the fundamentals of man-to-man defense as far as individual player's mechanics are concerned. To be an effective performer in any type of defense, your players must have mastered these fundamentals.

1. Study virtually every known defense to learn strengths and weaknesses of each. We believe in teaching our varsity practically every defense for use in just one early-season scrimmage session. We don't do this with offenses.

2. Pick your defenses and teach. We favor multiple defenses as much as we do a single offensive formation. For scrimmage sessions, stick to the half-court with the varsity playing all offense or all defense. Spend as much time on defense as on offense.

Plan practices: Plan your practices carefully in advance so as to include everything, especially preseason practices when you're doing your foundation teaching. Have a time schedule and follow it religiously. Even if you're not satisfied with performance in a certain part of practice, schedule more work on it another day—stick to the schedule.

> **NOTE: You should post the detailed schedule, including time allowed for every drill. Include your chalkboard time (remember you don't just teach how, but also why and when).**

Some practice pointers include:

1. Never put tactics ahead of fundamentals. This is partly why we recommend keeping tactics simple—to teach thoroughly without interfering with constant work on fundamentals.

2. Don't let any player regard himself as such a specialist that he is excused from mastering every fundamental.

> **EXAMPLE: That tall, clumsy kid who rebounds so well can hurt you with a crucial turnover if you let him ignore his dribbling deficiencies.**

3. Make every drill right from your offense and make the players know where and how the moves fit in—same for defense.

4. Have every offensive drill include shooting—regardless of what other fundamental you are emphasizing, such as the pivots, various dribbling moves, and passing. Never allow the shooting to become sloppy or in any way secondary to other parts of the drill.

Personal ideas: Here's a list of personal ideas that have worked for me through the years.

1. Strive for mastery of fundamental excellence rather than usual moves and shots. Think in terms of being smarter and sounder rather than

cuter. For instance, I preach that there is absolutely no margin for error in passing; a player risking a pass behind his back is done for the night—and at the bottom of the squad in standing.

> **NOTE: Value possession. Deplore anything contributing to turnovers. My ball handlers never try to beat a well positioned defensive man with the dribble. It's a team game and the most effective teams use the best judgment.**

2. The above is true of shooting as well. Work to create openings and clearance for good shots. Discourage shots forced through a defensive player. Allow no player to pass up good shots. The playground belief that passing off is a mark of cleverness can be overdone.

3. Young coaches are often carried away with training rules. You are a teacher—not a policeman. Keep rules few and simple. Make no threats you aren't prepared to back—and then apply them with no exceptions or favoritism.

4. Remember, it is the boys' team and their game. You and I are employed to help them do their best. Emphasize team membership as being of paramount importance. The word teammate is the most important word in the language. Protect that relationship.

5. Don't wase time on showmanship. I refer to intricate warm-up drills that are purely for warming up. There is too much basketball to be taught to spend valuable time teaching anything that won't be used in a ball game.

> **TIP: Why bother with drills that are solely for conditioning? If your boys are working hard in drills and scrimmage, conditioning comes automatically.**

6. Never say "don't do that again," without showing or explaining what to do. Many coaches get so involved with negatives that they do virtually nothing positive. Praise good performance just as much as you criticize mistakes.

2

Specialized Pressure Basketball: Offensive and Defensive Systems

by Ron Vlasin

Basketball Coach
Merino High School
Merino, Colorado

Ron Vlasin's six year coaching record at Merino High School is 90 wins, 23 losses. His teams hold the state record for consecutive wins with 46 straight. He has also coached his teams to two state championships and one state runner-up position.

Although we realize the value of a good all-around basketball player, we feel that today's high-speed game requires a great deal of specialization. Thus, after instructing our players in what we believe are the fundamentals of basketball, we teach each player only one position. If he can play this one position well, he can fit into our program and help our team.

Philosophy: Before detailing the specific positions in our system, we should make clear our philosophy of the game. We feel that to beat opponents, we must keep constant pressure on them, so that they are forced to play under steady pressure at a pace they are unaccustomed to. To keep our own players alert and aggressive, we attempt to maintain this pressure in as simple a manner as possible.

DEFENSIVE GAME: Defensively, we apply the pressure with a standard 3-1-1 full-court press. If the opposition

gets the ball upcourt against our press, we fall back into a tight man-to-man defense as our basic defense. Occasionally, we change to a zone when we feel that the opposition or situation warrants it.

Offensively, we try to keep constant pressure on the opposition by fast-breaking not only after missed shooting attempts and loose balls, but also, and especially, after made baskets. If we do not have the break, we go quickly into our offense.

Specific positions: Our positions are called by five specific names: short guard, deep guard, center, short forward, middle forward. Each of these positions requires a player to play a specific position offensively and defensively. This assignment never changes and is such that a player who fills the physical requirements for a position offensively will also possess the physical requirements for his defensive position.

> **NOTE: With this system, if we are forced to make a replacement for any reason, we do not have to adjust our offense, defense, or any of our players. The player entering the game will simply have the same assignments as the player he replaces.**

Diagrams 1 and 2, respectively, illustrate these five basic defensive press and offensive fast-break positions:

x^1—Deep Guard (side up-man defensively; deep guard offensively)

x^2—Center (center up-man defensively; out-of-bounds man offensively)

x^3—Short Forward (side up-man defensively; safety valve offensively)

x^4—Middle Forward (middle man defensively; middle man offensively)

x^5—Short Guard (short back-man defensively; outlet man offensively)

Characteristics and Assignments for
Each Position

Following are the individual characteristics and the basic offensive and defensive assignments for each of the five positions.

Deep guard: The deep guard position requires an excellent shooter. We hope this player will also be our tall guard, so that he can rebound if he has the chance to go one-on-one in a fast-break situation. *Offensively*, his job is to get down the floor as quickly as possible. Once he reaches his

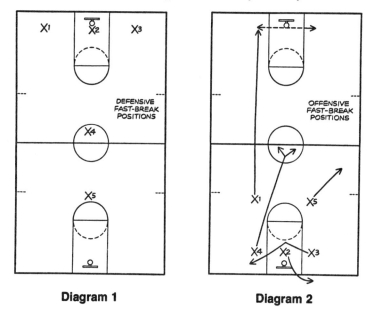

Diagram 1   **Diagram 2**

forecourt baseline, he breaks to either side of the floor to get open. If we can get him the ball, he has to go for the shot.

Defensively, this player is one of the side up-men on our press. His job is to prevent the inbounds pass to his side. If the ball gets inbounds, he must trap when it is to his side or shut off the nearest passing lane when it is to the opposite side.

Short guard: This position requires an excellent ball handler. He should also be quick, fast, and an excellent passer and dribbler. *Offensively,* his job is to break to the side of the floor near mid-court for the outlet pass and then get the ball upcourt as quickly as possible.

Defensively, he is the short end of our press. His job is to intercept any deep pass thrown. If he is faced with a 2-on-1 or a 3-on-1 situation, he must prevent an easy shot or try to stall for help.

Center: The center position must be filled by a tall player who is strong enough to throw deep, accurate passes. He should also be a good rebounder. *Offensively,* his job is to rebound and get the ball out to our short guard if the shot is missed. If the shot is made, he must take the ball out-of-bounds. His first inbounds choice is our deep guard; second choice, our short guard, and third, our middle forward. If all three of these men are covered, he gives the ball to our short forward, who is our safety valve. After any inbounds pass he makes, he must hustle hard to our offensive end of the court.

> **DEFENSE: On defense, this player is the up-tight man on our press. His job is to prevent a long, deep pass, or cause it to be wild. If the ball comes inbounds short, his assignment is to trap along with the up-man to the ball side.**

Middle forward: Your quickest, best ball-handling forward is needed at this position. He should be a good shooter and rebounder, too. *Offensively*, his job is to rebound and get the outlet pass to the short guard, and then fill the third lane. If the shot is made, he heads up the middle of the floor. If one of the guards gets the inbounds pass, he fills the third lane. If he receives a pass, he passes off to one of the guards as quickly as possible, then fills the third lane.

Defensively, he plays in the middle of our press. He must trap to the side of the ball if it gets past our up-man, or close to the nearest passing lane if the trap is made by our up-man, and try to intercept any intermediate pass.

Short forward: The man in the short forward position is usually our tallest, best-rebounding forward. Though he does not need great speed, he should be a fair ball handler with poise. *Offensively*, his job is to rebound and make the outlet pass. If a shot is made, he breaks to a short position to the opposite side from our short guard and serves as a safety valve. If he does not get the ball, he is a trailer on our fast break. When he does get the inbounds pass from our center, he holds it until our short guard comes back to get it from him.

> **DEFENSE: Defensively, the man in the short guard position plays as a side up-man. His job is to prevent the inbounds pass. When the ball does get inbounds, he must trap if it is to his side; shut off the nearest passing lane if it is to the other side.**

3

Offensive and Defensive Philosophy

by Bob Morgan

Head Basketball Coach
George S. Parker High School
Janesville, Wisconsin

Bob Morgan was head coach at Winneconne High School (Wisconsin) for five years before coming to Parker High School in 1968, when the school first opened. He was selected Big-8 "Coach-of-the-Year" in his first year at Parker. His 1970-71 team won the state championship and his 1971-72 team (rebuilt) again advanced to the state, placing fourth. He has never had a losing season in ten years of coaching and has an overall record of 164-65 for a .733 percentage. Coach Morgan was selected as the 1970-71 Wisconsin Prep Coach-of-the-Year.

At various basketball clinics I have been attending, there has been interest in our high school's offensive and defensive philosophy. It is a changing or multiple offense and defense that we used in winning the Wisconsin State basketball championship for the 1970-71 season. I present it here in some detail in the hope that it will benefit others.

Offensive Philosophy

Pre- and early season:
1. Have a good idea of capabilities and the potential varsity squad and

265

decide on the type of offense suited to meet the needs of your personnel.

2. Schedule your non-conference games to meet preconference and tournament needs.

3. A knowledge of opponent's defense and returning players may make a difference in your offense.

4. Potential players should be encouraged to participate in summer and fall programs. Have a weight training program and a conditioning program set up for all prospective players.

TIP: Keep in close contact with the players during the summer and fall. Be interested in them the entire year and not just during the basketball season.

5. At the opening of the season have a definite plan of evaluation of players for cutting purposes and give every player trying out a "good chance" to show his capabilities.

6. Use conditioning, ball-handling drills, three-on-three, and scrimmages to aid in determining cuts. In cutting keep in mind your junior varsity and sophomore roster. Don't keep players who you know will never play on the varsity.

NOTE: Seniors should be starters or first substitutes.

Multiple offense:

1. Have more than one type of offensive pattern. By having several offenses you force opponents to spend practice periods against all of them—provided they scouted the games in which all were used.

2. Scouting is made more difficult—an opponent may have scouted a game in which the offense was different from the one they will face.

3. Multiple offenses are excellent for tournament preparation or when you have little or no pregame information about an opponent's defense. You can switch quickly to an offense which would attack a certain defense the best.

4. Offenses should not be complicated. Players should understand the reason why a certain offensive pattern is to be used and have confidence in it.

5. Decide on the type of game you want to play.

FOR EXAMPLE: A fast-break game as the offensive weapon; a control type game where a team looks for a good percentage shot; fast break when the opportunity is there and if not, look for the good percentage shot.

6. A good offense is based on the players' poise, patterns, precision, and team play.

7. Have all five players moving on offense—movement without the ball is of vital importance.

8. Players should have a thorough understanding of the offense and should be able to play at all five positions.

9. Have a patterned offense with continuity—have rebounders in good board position and have good defensive balance.

10. Have enough options off the pattern to allow for individual freedom to run options.

11. Stress team offensive effort and do not allow any forced shots.

12. While working on offense demand perfection of movement of all players and correct every careless mistake—especially during half-court and full-court scrimmages.

13. Stress timing of passes, picks, cutting, etc. Demand excellence even if mistakes are of a minor nature.

14. Try not to have an offense revolve around one or two individuals. Foul trouble, injuries or illness may sideline them.

15. Be honest with your players. Let them know exactly what you expect of each individual and how they fit into the offense. Point out their strengths and weaknesses.

16. Drills used during practice sessions should be carefully thought out so they blend in with the offensive movement and individual efforts.

17. Make the defense adjust to your offense rather than you trying to adjust to the opponent's defense. By having a multiple offense you can easily move into any one of them after a look at the defensive alignment.

18. A good defense can be your best offense.

Develop offensive opportunities from:

1. Several offenses—the team may use only one an entire game or may use as many as four.

2. Out-of-bounds plays.

3. Fast-break offense.

4. Stall offense.

5. Offense against the press.

6. Last-second offensive plays.

7. Free throws.

8. Off jump balls.

9. Offensive rebounds.

10. Offense off the defense—full-court pressure; half-court pressure; tipping zones.

NOTE: Some basic offensive alignments are shown in: Diagram 1 (double stack); Diagram 2 (single stack); Diagram 3 (3 out); Diagram 4 (2-1-2 post).

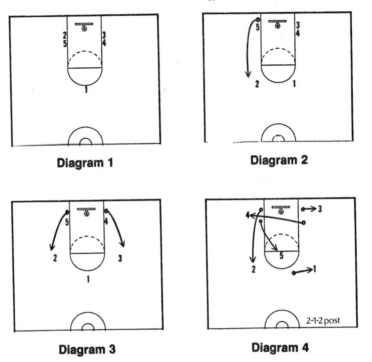

Diagram 1   **Diagram 2**

Diagram 3   **Diagram 4**

Defensive Philosophy

The defense:

1. Equal emphasis should be placed on defense because a team may have an "off night" offensively and still win because of a tough defense.

2. A player's instinct is for offensive basketball—players learn this at an early age. Not often does an individual concentrate on holding another player to a few points. Consequently, most players are weak on man-for-man defense and the offensive player has an advantage.

3. A good zone defense is best. A variety of well-executed zones is better, especially if you do not have a big man.

4. Determination, pride, and aggressiveness are keys to a good defense. Stress defense more than offense. The offense gets enough publicity and credit.

5. Have some type of an award for a game's outstanding defensive player based on a point system.

6. Place emphasis on: leading defensive rebounder; blocked shots; recovery of loose balls; steals; forcing of offensive fouls; stopping a high scorer; holding a team under their offensive average; pass interceptions; etc.

7. Build a reputation for being a good defensive team and pride will make the players continue this.

8. Stress avoiding foolish fouls caused especially by:

a) Giving up the baseline.

b) An outside shot.

c) Trying to take the ball away from an opponent in a one-on-one situation.

d) Making a mistake.

e) Not having the inside position for rebounding.

f) Reaching in because of being out of position.

9. Types of fouls permitted should be caused by contact while:

a) Going after a loose ball.

b) Trying to intercept a pass.

c) Blocking out.

d) Inside fouls on mismatch or shot-blocking attempt.

e) Occasional offensive foul.

10. Develop several zone defenses and presses.

11. Players should have a thorough understanding of the different defenses and be able to adjust from one to another without confusion by any player.

12. Players should be able to play any of the five positions.

Advantages of using zone defenses:

1. Reduces the number of fouls.

2. Can easily switch a player in foul trouble without hurting the defense.

3. Forces opponents to play a different game from the one they would like to play.

4. Using different zones or making a zone look like a man-for-man can confuse an opponent.

5. Opponents will have to spend practice time against all types of zones and presses while preparing for you.

6. Once the opponent feels it has solved one zone you can employ another type of defense.

7. If a team has scouted you they may not have seen the type of defense that will be used against them. Surprise element.

8. Helps control the tempo of the game because it is harder to penetrate.

9. Stops a driving team and upsets a team that is impatient or likes to take the quick shot.

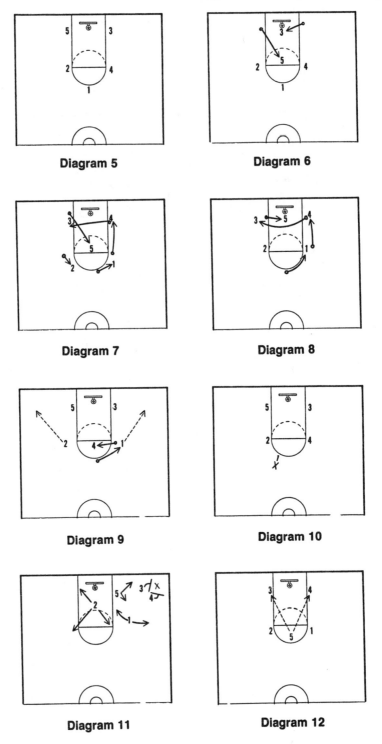

Diagram 5

Diagram 6

Diagram 7

Diagram 8

Diagram 9

Diagram 10

Diagram 11

Diagram 12

10. Can fast break easier and more effectively because the players are in the most advantageous positions.

11. Keeps individual strengths and weaknesses in the best positions——rebounders, small men, etc.

12. The ball can be played "tough" and you can double-team because you know you will have help should your man get by you.

13. Players cannot be "drawn out" of positions they play best or the small man cannot be caught on a mismatch underneath the basket.

14. You can use several zone presses and fall back into that zone defense without confusion.

15. Excellent in tournament preparation or when you have little or no pre-game information about an opponent's offense.

16. A good defense may be your best offer.

Multiple zone defenses:
1. The 1-2-2 zone (Diagram 5).
2. The 1-3-1 zone (Diagram 6).
3. The 2-1-2 zone (Diagram 7).
4. The 2-3 zone (Diagram 8).
5. The 1-2-2 with wing men covering the corners (Diagram 9).
6. The Box-and-1 or the Diamond-and-1 (Diagram 10).
7. The double-team from the above zones (Diagram 11).
8. The 3-2 zone (Diagram 12).
9. The match-up zone.
10. Zone presses—1-2-2; 1-3-1; 2-1-2; three-quarter and half-court presses.